Igniting Universal Empowerment

A RALLYING CRY FOR HUMANITY

Jen Ward
Marvin Schneider

Jarvin Media
Wodonga, Australia

Jen Ward & Marvin Schneider / Jarvin Media
https://www.jarvin.media/contact

Igniting Universal Empowerment/ Jen Ward & Marvin Schneider.

ISBN 978-0-6457789-0-8

Table of Contents

Front Matter

Foreword v

Welcome to Jarvin Media xix

The Chapters

A Rallying Cry for Humanity 1

Igniting Universal Empowerment 7

Universal Consciousness 17

The Human Collective 23

Waking to Awakening 29

Ascension Realized 41

Nature's Wisdom 51

Living a Spiritual Life 57

The SFT Tapping Protocols 61

Taps to Dissipate the Agents of Disempowerment

Autocrats, Dictators, and Powermongers 73

Political Divisiveness 79

The Drive to War 85

The Military Industrial Complex 91

Weapons of Mass Destruction 97

Conspiracy Theories 103

Secret Agendas 109

Extremism and Hate Fueled Violence 115

Inequality and Injustice 121

Poverty and Hunger 127

Overpopulation 133
Disease 141
Environmental Catastrophe 147
Earth as an Ashcan 155
Cults and Personality Worship 163
Religious Power Structures 169
Family Power Structures 175
The Daisy of Death 181
New Age Practices 187
The Universal Mind 195
The Ego 201
Wake the F@#k Up 207

*We dedicate this book to all those who have
incarnated in this life as advocates for truth.
Thank you for your lifetimes of sacrifice. You, who are
reading this now, are kindred spirits. Thank you for holding
space for the intentions we put forth.*

Truth and love resonate at similar frequencies.
If you want to experience more love in the world,
put a greater value on truth.

—JEN WARD

Foreword

It is such an honor to write this book as part of our mission to ignite universal empowerment. We, being Jen Ward and Marvin Schneider, have individually and collectively been on a journey of spiritual enlightenment and service to humanity for many, many lifetimes. Let's just say that this is not our first rodeo. And we are back at it again at this critical juncture of human evolution on planet Earth. Now is the time for all of us to awaken, become empowered, and to use that empowerment in the service of all of humanity.

That is why we have founded Jarvin Media. And that is why we work tirelessly to bring new, insightful, fresh, and compelling multi-media content to you. Because it is in the doing of these things that humanity will truly experience its divine providence of perpetual Abundance, Health, and Success, along with ultimate Joy, Love, Freedom, and Wholeness. This is our resolute intention.

We intend this book to be a seminal work that brings together the core tenets of human existence and purpose in a commonsense and accessible form. This knowledge forms the backbone of the Jarvin Media content that we produce. While there are a lot of books on related topics written by various gurus, sages, and wise people, many of them seem to us to be written in riddles. Our intention is that this book will be a straight shooter, providing truth, understanding, and foundational knowledge without fear or favor.

There is so much misunderstanding and even misinformation out there about the nature of human existence and its relationship to Source. This misunderstanding is why the better part of 8 billion people on the planet are separated from their own empowerment. Empowerment, when experienced on a large enough scale, is a precondition to the mass ascension of humanity.

That is why we have been compelled to write this book. It is critically important that a good proportion of the 8 billion people on the planet quickly progress along the ascension journey. Failure to do so will lead humanity down a dark path.

It is worth noting at this point that there are a lot of forces in the universe working tirelessly to put humanity onto a path of ascension and enlightenment. Those forces have been actively working towards this goal for the better part of this, the current epoch of sentient life on Earth. And so, it is important to know that we are not alone in this pursuit.

But it is also important to know that we cannot sit back and wait for alien Beings or other external forces to save humanity. We must do the work. You must do the work. There is no such thing as a free lunch! So, don't be fooled into complacency. The notion that we just have to wait for God or the Messiah to save us is part of the misunderstanding and misinformation that is holding humanity back from its own empowerment.

Empowerment. It is such an interesting word. And it is a core theme underpinning this book and the work we do. So, what does empowerment mean, and why is it so important?

From a dictionary definition perspective, empowerment is the process of becoming stronger and more confident, especially in controlling one's own life and claiming one's sovereignty. This is a pretty accurate account of what we mean by empowerment. However, we charge this phrase with the vibration of being the driver of your own path to enlightenment and your true sovereignty as a spiritual Being.

This is pretty heady stuff, right? Well, strap yourself in for the ride of your life! Because it just gets more interesting from here.

In the remainder of this book, we will be laying out the key elements of 'truth' from the vantage point of higher consciousness as we know it. But before we do that, it is worth addressing the topic of truth.

There is so much competition for information within this hyper social media fueled landscape. A lot of that information can be best described as misinformation, disinformation, and even 'fake news'. Some of it is innocent and just plain naïve. But a lot of it is orchestrated to push a particular agenda and world view. Often, those agendas are grounded in a specific nefarious intention to control, dominate, subjugate, or wield power over groups of people.

It is often hard to discern what is truth and what is just noise designed to keep us from truth. Every time you see, read, or hear something, ask yourself, "Who or what is behind the information? What is their motivation? And how does it empower me?" If the answers to these questions raise any red flags for you, perhaps it is best not to engage with the material. And if it puts you into a position of fear or powerlessness, it is certainly not from a source of higher consciousness.

The truth being offered in this book will no doubt shock and potentially offend some people. That is because some of the fundamentals of universal consciousness and human existence discussed in this book are completely at odds with the very tightly held views of billions of people that subscribe to mainstream religion. Even some of the ideas and practices offered by a lot of new age spiritual groups is either plain wrong or past their 'use by date'.

No doubt some people will ask "Who the hell are you to offer truth and question other people's truth?" Granted, we are perhaps not as well-known at this stage as Jesus, Mohamad, His Holiness the Dali Lama, Swami Muktananda, Sadhguru, Ekhart Tolle, or Deepak Chopra. But we have each experienced many lifetimes at various levels of enlightenment that have provided the perfect resume for formulating and communicating the truth that we are now offering to all of humanity. We are also heavily immersed in and guided by Source in all that we do.

This is not to say that others have not had many lifetimes at various levels of enlightenment, or are themselves not guided by Source. It is just that we seem to have a particular role to play in the ascension of humanity at this point in time. In a sense, we are simply fulfilling our purpose and destiny. So here, in the remainder of this foreword, we lay out some of those markers so that you can judge for yourself whether this truth resonates with you, and whether it is relevant to the ultimate goal of igniting universal empowerment.

We, being Jen and Marvin, are soulmates that are intimately connected in spirit. We have incarnated on this Earth at this point in time to play our part in igniting universal empowerment. We have had many lifetimes together in the pursuit of this purpose. And for the most part, we have failed for one reason or another. And so, we are back at it. We work tirelessly to set the conditions and create the tipping point for what many, many wayshowers have been alluding to – human transcendence from the third dimensional state of consciousness to the fifth dimension and beyond. It is finally time for humanity to come out of the dark ages once and for all.

While we are soulmates and have a bond grounded in a common purpose, we each have our own unique experiences, upbringing, capabilities, and role to play in this project.

Jen represents the female or Yin energy aspect of Source. She is a world-renowned energy healer who has a unique ability to perceive in energy, shift energy, and directly communicate with higher consciousness. This ability has been honed over many, many lifetimes. She is the anchor and inspiration for all things spiritual and intangible within Jarvin Media. She operates primarily in higher consciousnesses, outside of the constraints of time and space and the physical realms of existence.

Marvin represents the male or Yang energy aspects of Source. While he is very much grounded in the physical realms of existence, he has a strong ability to tap into direct knowingness and to translate intangible ideas into structures, plans, and action. He has had a number of lifetimes in significant leadership roles that have thrust humanity forward in profound, and at times unexpected ways. In his purest form, he holds the blueprint for realms beyond the fifth dimension. Together, Jen and Marvin build understanding and form around these higher realms so they can be accessed while in the physical body.

So, let's continue by more fully exploring Jen's soul story.

Jen has experienced significant challenges in this incarnation. She has come from the university of hard knocks. Her extraordinary and challenging personal journey includes being born to dysfunctional, poor, and alcoholic parents; being abused and deprived of any love and attention as a child; being overlooked and diminished for most of her adult life; and being locked up, starved, and tortured by a sociopath for a year. She truly has experienced almost every facet of the worst aspects of the human experience. You would not want to wish this onto even your worst enemy!

As tragic as these experiences are, they do set the scene for the amazing energy healing work she does in her compulsion to uplift all of humanity. This is because most people are carrying within their energy field, trauma and other core issues that are holding them back from experiencing their divine providence of perpetual Abundance, Health, and Success. It has also given her a unique ability to love all life – both animate and inanimate. Insomuch as her many past lives have prepared her for her current role, her experiences in this incarnation have sharpened her skills and abilities.

The fact that she was love and experience deprived as a child, and sensory deprived during her captivity, makes her additionally hyper-sensitive in energy. This level of hyper-sensitivity enables Jen to experience very intimate and personal relationships with a group of ancient, ascended masters known as the Adepts.

The Adepts operate near the inner sanctum of Source. Their role is to keep the universe functioning in an orderly manner. They are if you like, the designers, maintainers, and overseers of the universal blueprint. While they have transcended the need to take physical form, they will often incarnate and take corporeal form for the purpose of reconnecting themselves with dynamics of the lower worlds. What use are higher consciousness Beings if they have no sense as to the goings on in the lower worlds?

Jen's relationship with the Adepts is very special. They kept her alive, nurtured her, guided her, and helped her awaken to her own spiritual mastery that had been honed over many past lives. They continue to work with Jen to this day.

Jen has had several notable past lives and many tragic past lives that are relevant to this discussion. It is important to note that many people have had notable past lives. And most people have had many past lives as both the hero and the villain. Many of us have been involved in some of the most horrific acts in human history. No one is as pure as the driven snow. In fact, a belief that you are as pure as the driven snow is a form of denial.

Let's start with two notable lives that also involved Marvin. The first was as Olympias, the mother of Alexander III the Great. The second was as Morgana (also known as the Lady of the Lake) during the King Arthur of Camelot era.

Olympias was the wife of King Philip II of Macedonia and was the mother of Alexander III the Great. She lived from 375 BC to 316 BC. In human history, this was a time of great intellectual and political enlightenment. But it was also a time of empire building, conquest, and destruction. Such is the extreme level of duality that is prevalent across the full spectrum of the human experience.

Aside from the historical and geopolitical context of that lifetime, Olympias was a woman of great diversity and complexity. She was born into royalty and was part of the privileged elite. She was a power player, politician, diplomat, and schemer. She was responsible for executing xii | Jen Ward & Marvin Schneider

many of her enemies. She was exiled several times. She was demonized. But she mostly acted with the noble intention of being of service to her people.

This was a lifetime in which Jen experienced firsthand the need to maintain female strength while reigning in and balancing the strongest urges of male energy. As the mother of Alexander, she was both responsible for elevating his sense of conquest and also for tempering his conquests to pursue a path of peace and diplomacy. In many respects, she ultimately failed in the latter pursuit. But this lifetime was important because it gave Jen a sense of the use and abuse of power in female energy. The abuse of power and the appropriate role of female Goddess energy are themes that are very close to Jen's heart.

One of the more controversial lifetimes that are prominent within Jen's akashic record is that of Morgana during the King Arthur era. This lifetime is controversial for several reasons, not least of which is that there is no solid evidence of King Arthur from a historical perspective. But the legend and folklore of King Arthur persists even to this day. And many people have a strong association with King Arthur, Camelot, Avalon, Excalibur, the Knights of the Round Table, the Holy Grail, Merlin, Lancelot, and so on. The fact that so many people associate with the legend makes it real in energy on some level. The other reason this lifetime is controversial is that Morgana was demonized in popular myth, whereas in truth, she was the unsung hero. Whenever there is a woman demonized in popular culture, know there is a deeper truth to the matter.

The significance of the Arthur era is that it was meant to usher in a time of peace, harmony, and higher consciousness by bringing male and female Goddess energy back into balance. The stage had been set for this outcome. All the pieces had been carefully positioned on the chessboard. But there was a spoiler plot in the midst, and humanity was plunged into nearly a thousand years of further darkness. Which just goes to show that in as much as the Adepts work to create the circumstances for a particular outcome, there is still freewill. All possible realities are in play in all moments. The observed reality is the one in which there is the greatest weight of intention.

Morgana was slated to play a very significant role during the Arthur era. She was highly skilled at perceiving in energy - much more than Merlin. And despite her being his half-sister, Morgana was destined to marry Arthur and rule Camelot with him to bring universal empowerment and higher consciousness to the world. Importantly, Morgana was destined to play the traditional Goddess role. Her wisdom and his strength were meant to be fused together to elevate consciousness.

Let's just say that things didn't quite work out as planned. To begin with, black magic was used to trick Arthur into falling in love with Guinevere. But the nails in the coffin were firstly Lancelot's betrayal of Arthur as a result of his affair with Guinevere; and secondly, Morgana's banishment from Camelot. These sorry events prevented Camelot from fulfilling its true purpose. Humanity was kept in the dark ages and the universal grand plan for an era of Lemurian style spiritual enlightenment was foiled. So, the Adepts continued to quietly work in the background to set the scene for another attempt at universal empowerment.

Morgana's banishment from Camelot set the scene for Jen to have dozens of lifetimes of truly horrible and deplorable experiences. For example, Jen has conscious recall of being an untouchable in India. There, she lived in poverty and filth, eating putrid scraps discarded by those of the higher casts. She also has conscious recall of being buried alive in one lifetime, and having her organs xiv | Jen Ward & Marvin Schneider

harvested by an alien race to create an army of cyborg-human cross breeds.

This pattern of banishment was finally broken during Jen's lifetime as Madame Helena Blavatsky. Madame Blavatsky was a historically significant figure that brought Eastern spirituality and occultism to the Western world. She was born into a wealthy aristocratic family in Dnipro, Ukraine in 1831. She was largely self-educated and travelled widely as a child. At the age of 18, she embarked on a series of world travels visiting Europe, America, and India. It was during these travels that she met a group of spiritual Adepts. She spent many years under their tutelage in Tibet where she refined her understanding of spirituality, religion, philosophy, and science.

Madame Blavatsky founded the Theosophical Society in New York City in 1875 with the aim of reviving an ancient wisdom that had been lost and buried within mainstream Western religion. She was a controversial figure. She was championed by her supporters as an enlightened sage and derived by her critics as a charlatan. Nevertheless, her Theosophical doctrines influenced the spread of Hindu and Buddhist ideas to the West.

There are several important themes that stem from the Blavatsky experience. One was the way in which Blavatsky's ideas were hijacked by others. This theme is expressed in a number of ways. Firstly, she was pushed out of the Theosophical Society by some of her closest confidants. Secondly, her work was the core inspiration for a religious cult known as Eckankar. And thirdly, several nefarious characters in history used some of Blavatsky's ideas for their own perverted purposes. Adolf Hitler is a prime example of this. In a lot of ways, Jen is continuing the work of Madame Blavatsky in this life. She is also committed to correcting the distortions of her work from the Blavatsky lifetime.

One of Jen's other notable lifetimes was as an Essene during the time of Jesus. The Essenes were a mystical Jewish sect that flourished from the fifth century BC to the first century AD. As a sect of mystics, they sought a direct and personal experience of the divine. They understood that the spiritual world transcends the physical world. Many were skilled in the art of perceiving in energy. Jen was one such Essene.

During that lifetime, Jen was a female energy healer who taught Jesus the healing arts during his 'forty days' in the desert. She was also very close to Mary Magdalene. She describes Mary Magdalene as a spiritual adept and as having a significant amount of influence over Jesus' teachings. In her recollection of that time, Jesus' importance was due to him being Mary Magdalene's husband and soul mate. This is in stark contrast to the portrayal of Mary Magdalene as a prostitute and a repentant sinner. It is another example of where the role of Goddess has been diminished and written out of history in favor of elevating the role of the male counterpart.

These are just a few of the past life experiences that Jen has conscious recall over. Marvin on the other hand does not have conscious recall of his past lives. Those described here were identified by either Jen or another intuitive that Marvin has worked with in the past. The defining theme underpinning these lifetimes is the experience and ultimate rejection of the abuse of power in favor of universal empowerment.

The stage was set for this theme to play out during Marvin's life as Alexander III the Great. Alexander conquered a vast empire that stretched from Greece in the West to Syria and Egypt in the South, and Eastwards to the border of India.

But in as much as there were ambitions to create a grand civilization that unified the peoples of much of the known world at the time, it came at the cost of a great deal of death and destruction. And it did not last beyond Alexander's short life. Alexander died a mere 12 years after becoming king of Macedonia and embarking on his conquest.

The real lesson to be learnt from Alexander's conquest and the many other attempts at empire building throughout human history, is that the use and abuse of power cannot and will not ultimately succeed. People's desire for personal sovereignty is much stronger than the ability of power mongers to exert their will over others.

In a lot of ways, this lesson created the condition for Marvin's experience of the King Arthur era as recalled by Jen. Arthur sought to undo the damage caused by Alexander by empowering others. His establishment of The Knights of the Round Table and their oath of service above all else is a great example of this. Even Arthur himself was not above the law. His undoing in that lifetime was that he trusted others too much to hold and carry the mantle of higher consciousness.

The last of Marvin's past lives worth mentioning here is that of the Nobel prize winning scientist, Lord Baron Ernest Rutherford. Rutherford was born in 1871 and was raised in a small rural community in New Zealand. His early education was basic. But he exceled at university and was accepted to complete his postgraduate studies at Cambridge, England. Many years later, he took over as the head of the Cavendish Laboratory at Cambridge University from his mentor J. J. Thomson.

He and his team did the ground-breaking experimental work to identify the structure of atoms – protons, neutrons, and electrons. This discovery was instrumental in defining the periodic table of elements which is the backbone of modern-day chemistry. It was also instrumental in the development of nuclear physics, nuclear energy, and of course the atom bomb. Towards the end of his life, Rutherford warned against the risks of nuclear energy and the potential to use his discoveries for creating weapons of mass destruction. Of course, the rest is history. Rutherford died in 1936 prior to the outbreak of World War II and the development of the first atomic bomb. As far as we can tell, the Rutherford life was Marvin's immediate prior life to his current incarnation.

So here we are again, doing our bit to uplift all of humanity and perhaps make right all the misadventure from our prior lives. We are not the only ones doing the work for the ascension of humanity. But we are the only ones doing it by coming together as polar opposites, and by synergizing our purposes to inspire mass awakening and to ignite universal empowerment.

We trust that you will get on board with us to become empowered, to experience perpetual Abundance, Health, and Success, and to add your synergy to the mass ascension process.

With the deepest love and respect,
Jen & Marvin
February 2023

Welcome to Jarvin Media

We have had an active social media presence for many years as part of the Jenuine Healing brand. But in early 2023, we got the nudge to launch a new brand with a mission of igniting universal empowerment and promoting perpetual Abundance, Health, and Success. The Jarvin Media branding elements reflect this intention.

JARVIN MEDIA

Igniting Universal Empowerment
ABUNDANCE ✴ HEALTH ✴ SUCCESS

We are creating within Jarvin Media an extensive catalog of online content including:

- A collection of videos containing 'relevant to the day' messages from Jen. You can think of these as your daily dose of inspiration to keep you grounded in your spiritual life.

- A collection of visualization videos. You can think of these as your upgrade to meditation.

- A collection of videos featuring tender and light-hearted moments of Jen and Marvin going about their business as part of them living their spiritual life.

- A collection of interviews in which Jen and Marvin discuss the spiritual journey experienced by various special guests.

- A collection of videos dedicated to teaching you how to release and overcome the core issues and conditions faced by most of the 8 billion people on the planet. You can think of these as removing all blockages to your self-healing.

- A collection of recordings of Jen working with clients during private healing sessions. Being part of these healings is a great way to heal yourself as well.

- A collection of topic relevant videos dedicated to answering the burning questions that people have about spirituality and the nature of human existence. You can think of these as your spiritual knowledge primers.

- A collection of intensive workshops facilitated by Jen and Marvin dedicated to providing you with practical and tangible information and skills. You can think of these as your spiritual master classes.

- A collection of livestream recordings in which Jen and Marvin facilitate healings in a group setting.

- A collection of livestream recordings in which Jen and Marvin facilitate group SFT tapping sessions focused on addressing core issues at the level of the collective.

- A collection of weekly Satsang livestream recordings with Jen and Marvin. Think of these events as tapping into your omniscience, omnipresence, and omnipotence.

- Direct access to Jen through the online Jarvin Media community. Think of this as a way for you to add your voice to Jarvin Media content.

Some of this content will be available for free on the Jarvin Media YouTube, Instagram, Facebook, LinkedIn, and podcast channels. However, most of the content will only be accessible on a subscription basis or on a pay-per-view basis. You can become a member of the Jarvin Media online community by signing up for one of the subscription packages that we are offering.

Our objective is for Jarvin Media to be the pre-eminent and authoritative source of practical and actionable knowledge, insights, tools, skills, and techniques for spiritual awakening and living a spiritual life. We are here to raise consciousness one individual at a time, and then snowball that into igniting universal consciousness. We are here to help you live and thrive in the fifth dimension rather than just striving to get there. And we have created a safe and inclusive online community for those who are on a spiritual path. Our intention is that Jarvin Media will be your portal to higher consciousness.

Please join us at https://jarvin.media.

CHAPTER 1

A Rallying Cry for Humanity

Humanity is facing some pretty significant challenges. Many of these challenges have existed for most of this epoch of human history. Some of them arise from more recent human inventions, technologies, and institutions. But either way, their existence stems from a low level of human consciousness that is disconnected from Source. And their resolution is grounded in universal empowerment.

As we were preparing to write this chapter of the book, we were in two minds as to whether to put attention on the negative aspects of the human experience. The more you put attention on something, the more you are grounding it in your own reality, and ultimately the lived experience of the collective.

But it is equally not helpful to be completely naïve as to the existence of these things. We believe the correct balance is to acknowledge them in a way that doesn't feed them, and then immediately work to address the issues from a higher vantage point.

A lot of people are very passionate about their pet issues. Passion and anger are a step up from apathy. That is a good thing. But the combination of these emotions often perpetuate issues rather than resolve them. This is particularly true when the issues are highly partisan in nature.

For the better part of modern history, major democracies have been founded on the two-party system, the left, and the right. Each side of the political spectrum represents opposite ideals and values. And yet the political discourse has been at least respectful for the most part. But have you noticed how that discourse has become more polarized, extreme, and downright nasty recently?

Extreme partisanship is a feature of current political and social discourse. It is being fueled by social media, and it is being increasingly weaponized. Social media has been hijacked by proponents of extreme positions on both sides of the social and political spectrum. It tends to anchor people in one side of an issue or the other. It promotes tribalism – 'us' versus 'them'. And it isolates people from exploring paths of common ground. All of this is a total distraction from our ultimate purpose, which is to experience ourselves as an aspect of Source.

There are so many pressing ecological, social, and political issues that we as a collective need to urgently act upon. Climate change. Pollution. Soil degradation. Extinction of wildlife and plant life. Over population. Hunger. Disease. Inequality. Hate fueled violence. Authoritarianism. Economic collapse. Protectionism. War.

All of these issues are man-made. All of them are solvable. All of them have a profound impact on each of the 8 billion people on this planet either directly or by putting limitations on an otherwise limitless level of Abundance, Health, and Success. And none of these issues are new.

So, if they are old issues and they personally impact everyone on the planet, why has so little progress been made on their resolution?

Some people may argue that the persistence of these issues is akin to mosquitos in the back yard while you are barbequing – a bit annoying, but ultimately bearable. We disagree. A combination of economic pressure points, a desire for super-powers to control and dominate scarce resources, and the rise of autocrats and dictators, is putting humanity on a very dangerous trajectory. Failure to address these issues in our lifetime will take humanity down a very dark path.

The root cause of all of these issues is a prevalence of regressive consciousness. Greed, self-interest, and being disconnected from the collective, nature, and universal consciousness are at the heart of all of these issues. The resolution is to operate from a position of higher consciousness. And the path to higher consciousness is the pursuit of universal empowerment.

No substantial progress will be made on these issues in the absence of universal empowerment. Our observed reality is the one in which there is the greatest weight of intention. That is why it is so important for a large proportion of the 8 billion people on the planet to awaken and put their intention behind universal empowerment.

One of Marvin's life purpose projects is to ignite the transformation of the global business and investment communities to create wealth on an ongoing basis in ways that enhance the wellbeing of the individual, the wider community, and the environment. In simple terms, it is to shift the cogs in the wheels of the collective from taking to outflowing.

If ever there was a need to raise the consciousness of a sub-section of the wider community, it would be that of big businesses and investment firms. This is because up until now, they have been programmed and conditioned to operate at a low level of consciousness to the detriment of the wider community and the environment.

The business and investment communities constitute an important part of society. Their actions and activities have a profound impact on individuals, the wider community, and the environment – either for better or for worse. So, it makes sense that a concerted effort should be made to raise the consciousness of the business and investment communities as part of the overall effort to uplift all of humanity.

There will be many readers of this book who have experience at a leadership level in big business. For those in this position, we have a specific call to action for you. You have a moral obligation to become part of the ecosystem of individuals and organizations driving change. The days of passing the buck are over.

All businesses need to create wealth. If they do not, they will cease to exist. The creation of wealth is both necessary and encouraged. The real questions are: how much wealth should be created; how should that wealth be created; and how do individuals, the wider community, and the environment benefit from the creation of that wealth?

There is only one way to create wealth on an ongoing basis in any fundamental sense. It is to institutionalize a mindset and a capability from the boardroom to the shop floor which is grounded in a noble intent to enhance the wellbeing of the individual, the wider community, and the environment.

But why is it so important to focus on enhancing the wellbeing of the individual, the wider community, and the environment through the company's activities? Simply put, if you do not, shareholders will increasingly not invest in your company; consumers won't buy your products and services; and regulators will step in and impose increasingly higher costs and sanctions.

Marvin has been quietly working on this agenda since 2012. He has developed all the understandings, frameworks, tools, and capabilities required to underpin the transformation process. But the necessary change cannot take place with the same low level of consciousness that created the problem in the first place. Change requires the fortitude, courage, and commitment of those in a position to influence. Our intention is that his book will jolt business leaders out of a state of apathy and into a state of higher consciousness so that they can drive the change process.

But it is not necessary for you to sit and wait in apathy for business leaders to be jolted into higher consciousness. There are some very tangible things that you can do right now to facilitate this change. Choose wisely what you consume and how much you consume. Buy less and buy goods of a higher quality. Disconnect from social media channels that abuse your data and privacy. Buy organic foods. Burn less fuel. Take fewer overseas holidays. Shun companies and supply chains that willfully exploit their workers or the environment. Buy locally if you can. And if you can't, ask yourself whether you need the item at all.

There is no greater motivator for change than the survival instinct. When you and billions of other people around the world change their consumption patterns in favor of companies that enhance societal wellbeing, even the most self-interested business leader will be forced to come onboard. And then you will have the pleasure of saying, "About time!"

In the next chapter, we will lay out the pathway to universal empowerment. And it all begins with individual empowerment. Yes, that means you.

CHAPTER 2

Igniting Universal Empowerment

Universal empowerment is a state of existence in which the collective has the lived experience of perpetual Abundance, Health, and Success. It is a state in which individuals live in harmony with each other and with nature, free from the man-made shackles that disempower people. It is a state in which you experience yourself as an eternal soul and an aspect of Source, intimately connected to universal consciousness.

While the goal is universal empowerment, mass awakening, and the ushering of the collective into higher consciousness, this process starts with you. So, for the majority of this section, we will be focusing on your empowerment.

There are so many ways in which you are disempowered. Most people are desensitized to the agents of disempowerment all around them. They have become so used to it that they don't even recognize when and how it is occurring. That stops right now.

In this chapter, we will be calling out ideas, conventional wisdom, institutions, groups, and archetypes that are either actively or subtly working against your own empowerment.

This will be a challenging experience for some people. This is because they have been so programmed and are so heavily vested in their tightly held world view, that it cuts them deep to their core to challenge it. Their ego will vehemently fight against any alternative understanding. We, being Jen and Marvin, have each experienced this reaction firsthand many times. But to not address these issues would be to shy away from our core purpose of igniting universal empowerment.

So, let's start with the least controversial archetypes of disempowerment - autocrats, dictators, and power mongers. These individuals seek and crave power for the gratification of their own ego. Their primary goal is to exert their will over the will of the collective. And they often reside at the head of brutal regimes supported by their hand chosen henchmen. But here is the thing. While they retain power through the exercise of fear and brutality, their real power is sourced in energy. They feed off the fear energy of the people they control.

What is interesting to us is that these regimes still exist in this day and age. As flawed as democracy is, particularly in this age of extreme partisanship, there really is no place for autocrats, dictators, and power mongers. They are a danger to the collective. And their mere existence holds the collective in a state of disempowerment. So, what can we do about them?

In the same way that autocrats, dictators, and power mongers are fed in energy through fear, apathy, and indifference, their downfall and demise will be crystalized in energy. But not by them being targeted with black magic. The key is to remove your energy from them; to break down their masks, walls and armor; and to shine a light on the illusion of untouchable power that they have created.

These kinds of people cannot stand being derided, diminished, or exposed for their pathetic petulance. They are no different than high school bullies with very fragile egos. As soon as you stand up to them in energy, watch how quickly they fall. This type of action is the ultimate form of mass civil disobedience. All you need to do is to channel your inner Gandhi.

Jen and Marvin have been doing the work to evaporate the energy from autocrats, dictators, and power mongers for many years. We have facilitated many group SFT tapping sessions focused on this task. We encourage you to add your synergy to this effort. There is no room for complacency. Because your silence and failure to act creates a psychic energy of apathy that is harnessed by power mongers. And even if you are not directly affected by the brutality of an autocratic regime, you are indirectly and very personally being affected through the geopolitical tensions that they create.

We don't always immediately see the cause and effect of our group SFT tapping sessions. It seems that a stock of energy needs to be put out into the universe before we witness change. This is because our observed reality is the one in which there is the greatest weight of intention. You have got to put a weight of intention out there. Having said that, it is always gratifying to observe the extent to which the illusion, walls, masks, and armor are being stripped off these individuals. There are autocrats, dictators, and power mongers the world over who are being exposed for what and who they are. Let's keep up the pressure!

Cult leaders and celebrities are another archetype that disempower people by taking energy from their followers. The thing about this group is that their followers and fans willing give away their energy through their adoration and devotion. Their exulted status depends on the continual feeding of energy in this way. But something seems to happen amongst this group of people. After a while of being at the top of their game, they tend to do some really stupid and bizarre things. It is like their egos go into overdrive. They just can't help themselves. Watch how quickly they fall from grace when they cross the red line.

As much as this group of disempowerment agents tend to get hoisted on their own petard, you don't need to wait for this to happen to get your empowerment back. The best thing to do is to avoid being trapped into cult, hero, or celebrity worship in the first place. But if you do find yourself trapped in a cult, or habitually worshiping a guru, saint, icon, or celebrity, do the SFT taps to disconnect in energy and to get your empowerment back.

A lot of people aspire to be famous, well known, and admired. There is nothing wrong with fame per se. But wouldn't it be better to be famous for what you offer humanity rather than being a taker in energy?

It would be wrong of us not to tackle the insidious and disempowering nature of hate-filled extreme ideology and the way that such ideology gets expressed in violence. The fuel for hate-filled extreme ideology is a sense of separation from the collective and the perpetuation of an 'us' versus 'them' narrative. We are not separated from the collective. We are all atoms of Source. We are all connected in energy as part of Universal Consciousness.

The antidote to extremism is for you to not identify with tribes. You are a sovereign Being in your own right. Your identity is not tied to your ethnicity, nationality, gender, or religious affiliations. You are a citizen of the universe. Being empowered means not giving over your sovereignty or loyalty to outside sources and influences.

But how do we deal with the extremism observed in others? Should we bear arms to defeat extremist threats? Our sense is that the use of force for self-defense can be justified in the short-term. The challenge is to ensure that the force is used with a pure and noble intention and in proportion to the threat. Too often, force used for self-defense takes on a life of its own and is then used to serve a broader, less pure, or less noble intention.

The practical reality is that the use of force has never been a long-term solution. The only long-term and sustainable solution is to lift the consciousness of the collective to reject extreme ideology all together.

Rampant and excessive consumerism is a powerful agent of disempowerment. The drive to consume is not only detrimental to the planet, but it also turns you into a slave to advertising. Advertising is a billion-dollar industry designed to manipulate you into consuming more than you need. Advertisers tap into the primal human urges of greed, need, and want. They are masters at it. You are giving up your precious empowerment to master manipulators every time you open yourself up to the suggestive messaging in advertising.

While advertising is mostly just plain manipulative, another more subtle form of manipulation is either being forced or expected to conform to societal norms. Keeping up with the Jones. White picket fences. The mortgage. Peer pressure. Patriotism. Career progression. College education. Marriage. Mom, dad, and the two kids. Loving your parents and siblings.

Jen has done hundreds of private sessions over the years helping clients regain their empowerment from the need to comply with social norms. If you feel disempowered by these forces, do the SFT taps to disconnect your energy from them and get your empowerment back.

Let's deal briefly with the one percent and how they stack the cards in their favor to the detriment of the ninety nine percent. As if rampant inequality is not bad enough, the one percent feel they are the 'masters of the universe' and are entitled to 'use the system' to retain and increase their power, wealth, and influence. The one percent become agents of disempowerment when their abuse of wealth puts limitations on the Abundance, Health, and Success of the collective.

A lot of people in America applaud the wealthy and the system that got them wealthy in the hope that they too will be wealthy one day. There is nothing wrong with wealth and abundance per se. We should add that from a spiritual perspective, abundance encompasses many more things than just monetary wealth. The key questions to ask and answer for yourself are: how much wealth is enough; how should that wealth be acquired; and how does the collective benefit from that wealth?

Of course, there are a number of wealthy families that are also philanthropists. This is great to a degree. But have you noticed how little progress has been made on fundamental issues despite the billions of philanthropic dollars being thrown at them? Yes, trillions of dollars are required to address systemic social and economic issues. But throwing money at problems is not enough. We need to address social and economic crises from a higher vantage point. That means, we need to raise the consciousness of the collective, including those in a position of power and influence.

We should give a brief shout out to the disempowering nature of conspiracy theories and the purveyors of such theories. While there are often some elements of truth to conspiracy theories, most of them contain a fair degree of misinformation and disinformation. People who crave truth will often venture into looking for conspiracy theories. A soul is captured by conspiracy theories when it is offered an element of truth that opens up their energy field. The real problem is that conspiracy theories rarely provide an uplifting path forward. They hold people in fear, judgement, and suspicion. They promote an 'us' versus 'them' mentality. Putting your attention on them, and then passing them on, just adds fuel to the fire.

If you want to do something about the deep state, false flag operations, the illuminati, the secret brotherhood, the petrodollar, the appropriation of alien technologies for covert purposes, or the military industrial complex, do the SFT taps on the issue.

But the big daddy of modern-day disempowerment is mainstream organized religion. There is no doubt that some valid sentiments and messaging exist within mainstream religious dogma. And mainstream religious institutions no doubt served a useful purpose at some point in human history. But some of the practices and core tenets of mainstream religion are holding people from their own sovereignty and empowerment. At a minimum, they are well past their 'use by date'. So, let's address some of them here.

The first is the institutionalization of religion itself. Their structures, hierarchies, rules, norms, expectations, and practices are either designed to, or in any case unintentionally, place you into a position of subservience. You are locked into being a part of the flock. But your sovereign connection to Source and to higher consciousness does not rely on you being part of a group structure. In fact, being part of a group structure is probably more of a hindrance than an aide. This is because any man-made structures, hierarchies and institutions ultimately get hijacked by the egos of those in a position of authority. To the extent that you benefit from the support and fellowship of others of a similar persuasion, feel free to participate in the Jarvin Media online community. At least it will not impose a power structure on you.

The second element of disempowerment is the notion of prayer, devotion, or worship to a higher authority outside of yourself. The truth is, there is no higher authority outside of yourself. So, when you genuflect in prayer to a God outside of yourself, you are really invalidating who you are as an aspect of Source itself. The interesting thing is that Jesus and many of the Christian Archangels, particularly Archangel Michael, do not want to be worshipped in this way. They are tired of being exulted to a higher position. This is because they know the truth of disempowerment through their worship.

Perhaps the biggest agent of disempowerment associated with Abrahamic religions (Judaism, Christianity, and Islam) is the rejection of reincarnation and the notion that your salvation can only be gained by adhering to their core teachings. The idea that you only have one life and one shot at salvation is extremely limiting and disempowering. It locks you out of exploring yourself as an eternal soul which is an aspect of Source having many incarnated experiences for the purpose of expanding universal consciousness.

It is critically important that all of the agents of disempowerment discussed in this section are resolutely and immediately defeated. There are two very tangible things you can do in this regard. The first thing you can do is to take care of your own sovereignty and empowerment. This requires constant vigilance and work. The second thing you can do is to participate in the energy work and group SFT tapping sessions that Jen and Marvin facilitate on a regular basis.

Something really magical happens when people first wake up to the expansive truth of universal consciousness and empowerment. Their whole universe is expanded in an instant. It sends them down a path of seeking and discovery. They suddenly realize that everything they thought they knew is a distraction, an illusion, a limitation. And then the real work begins.

As important as it is to prompt the 'wake-up moment' in yourself and the other 8 billion people on the planet, it is equally important that you and others do the work to progress along the spiritual path. Many people in the new age spiritual community get a sense of empowerment early in their awakening process, and then get lost in the chaos of re-examining everything they know about life and the universe. Some become quite unbalanced. Some get lost in their ego and become spiritual elitists. Some become slaves to mindless spiritual practices. Some get tangled in conspiracy theories. Others become captive to channeling their spirit guides.

While some or all of these things can be empowering for a period of time, it is important that you don't get lost in the mental aspects of them or become hostage to the 'daisy of death'. It is important to explore the full dimensions of your own omniscience, omnipresence, and omnipotence without getting lost in the ego or its esoteric nature. We have created the Jarvin Media online community to help you navigate through this process and towards your own empowerment.

.

CHAPTER 3

Universal Consciousness

More and more people are contemplating the really big questions as every day goes by. What is the nature of universal consciousness? What is the meaning of life? Why does life exist at all? And what is our role in the grand design of the universe, such as it is?

Unfortunately, there are still billions of people on the planet that have either never contemplated these questions or are resolute in the idea that there is no higher purpose at all. For them, life is all about getting as much as possible for themselves during their short tenure on Earth, even if it is achieved at the expense of others. Greed, the accumulation of wealth and power, self-interest, and indifference are their tools of trade. If you are at this end of the spectrum, perhaps these writings will give you a moment of pause and trigger within you the kind of 'holy shit' moment that seems to be common to all those awakening.

Then there are the billions of people who have a sense of some form of universal consciousness, but who are captive to the dogma surrounding mainstream religions or other forms of spiritual practice. This entrapment holds them in lower consciousness and prevents them from realizing themselves as omniscient, omnipresent, and omnipotent Beings. It is what Jen calls being trapped in the 'daisy of death.' If you are in this predicament, perhaps these writings may give you an opportunity to subtly shift vantage point and reclaim your sovereignty.

In this chapter, we will attempt to lay out, as best as we understand it, the nature of universal consciousness and our role in its grand design. This understanding is heavily influenced by the many lifetimes that Jen has had as a spiritually awakened soul.

As we gingerly navigate our way through these heady topics, we fully acknowledge that we do not have all the answers. We have become comfortable with the idea that there are some mysteries of the universe that will remain a mystery to us for as long as we choose to incarnate in a physical form. Being able to surrender to the idea of not knowing everything about the inner workings of the universe seems to be an important survival skill when living a spiritual life.

There is a lot of misinformation within the community at large, and even within the spiritual community, about the nature of universal consciousness and the purpose of life. And there is a lot of writing that can be best put in the category of platitudes – prosaic and poetic, but nonetheless trite and meaningless. While there may be a role for this kind of writing, we find that it doesn't fully serve the very practical and tangible needs of most of the 8 billion people on this planet who are struggling to make sense of it all.

To fill this void, we have constructed what we consider to be the core tenets of higher consciousness and spirituality in plain English. We hold these statements to be non-ambiguous and true to their fullest extent. While each of these statements are deliberately short and to the point, they contain within them layers and layers of richness that we explore and discuss with our Jarvin Media community. So, without further ado, here are the core tenets of universal consciousness as we understand them.

1. There is a universal consciousness. We will call it Source to avoid drawing upon the tainted concept of God.

2. We are spiritual beings whose consciousness exists beyond a single incarnated life. Most people alive on Earth right now have had many hundreds or thousands of incarnated lives, not all of which have played out on Earth.

3. As spiritual beings, we are an aspect of Source. We are interconnected in energy with everything in the universe, both animate and inanimate.

4. All individual atoms of Source possess awareness and are therefore conscious.

5. The purpose of an individual's life in its incarnated form is to realize itself as a conscious Being in its relationship to all other conscious Beings.

6. The purpose of life in its broadest perspective is to perceive life from every possible vantage point as a means to move the collective closer to Source.

7. The base nature of Source is love.

8. Gratitude and enthusiasm are the doorways to higher consciousness, whereas regret and apathy shut down opportunity.

9. The journey towards and beyond enlightenment never ends.

These core tenets speak to our identity as spiritual Beings that are an aspect of Source having a human experience for the purpose of expanding universal consciousness; and in the process, realizing ourselves as being an aspect of Source by piercing through the veil of separation that descends upon incarnation. Simple, right?

We think of Source as the primordial energy of the universe that is constantly in a state of flux, and which is perpetually organizing and reorganizing itself. This process of organizing and reorganizing energy creates experiences, memories, and imprints within the fabric of all of the energy that is contained within the universe. This process adds to the consciousness of the universe.

Trying to make sense of the origins of the universe is particularly challenging for us as we exist in a physical form. While it may not be technically accurate, it might be helpful to think of the origin of the universe as emanating from the big bang.

The big bang is that instant in time when all the energy that is and ever will be in the universe was ushered into physical existence. Since the time of the big bang, that energy has formed and transformed itself to create everything that is observable in the universe. Every atom that is observable in the universe has been transmuted from all the energy that was contained in the big bang.

And it gets more interesting. It is increasingly accepted within the scientific community that the universe we are currently experiencing is not the first big bang to have ever occurred, nor will it be the last. In fact, there is a view that we are currently experiencing the 84th incarnation of the physical universe. In this sense, the universe ebbs and flows, and creates and stores consciousness throughout its various journeys. But even within the 84th incarnation of the universe, there are still echoes of consciousness from previous incarnations.

Is there an intelligence responsible for each of the big bangs? Is there some kind of grand planner that orchestrates everything within each universe and between the universal ebbs and flows? To be honest, we have no idea. Various Hindu traditions give credence to Shiva filling this role, in which he brings about the destruction of one universe and 'roars' to usher in the big bang creation of the next universe.

We find it helpful to understand Source and the universe in terms of acquired consciousness rather than an orchestrating intelligence. This understanding is at odds with the 'intelligent design' view contained within many mainstream religions. We prefer the acquired consciousness understanding of the origins of the universe because it fits more naturally with the subtleties of the remaining tenets in which the purpose of Life is to expand the consciousness of the universe through experiences. It fits more naturally within the notion of free will and the exploration of souls in the universe as part of a pathway back to Source.

Of course, we are willing to concede that our conception of the origins of the universe may be wrong. For what it is worth, we do not find it practically helpful to explore the topic at a deeper level. We put this question in the category of the mysteries of the universe that will remain a mystery to us. In any case, there is enough richness in our current understanding to keep us busy for all the lives in which we chose to incarnate in the playground of this, the 84th incarnation of the universe.

For us, the most profound realization is that we are all spiritual Beings that are an aspect of Source having a human experience. Jen often describes us as being an emanation of light and a frequency of sound woven together in the illusion of form. In this sense, we are first and foremost energy. The trick for us having an incarnated human experience is to recognize ourselves as such. This is a really hard thing for most people to do. This is because most of us have very tangible experiences in the physical realm. To suggest that the physical world is an illusion seems absurd to many people.

There are some highly enlightened souls on Earth that can primarily experience themselves as energy in which the physical realm is an illusion. A guru sitting in the lotus position in a perpetual state of meditation may be an example of this phenomenon. Jen spends a lot of her time connected to Source in energy. That is why it is difficult for her to be grounded in the physical realm. Other people that are more attuned to their energy body also find it very difficult to function in the physical world.

There is so much to explore within these core tenets that it is not possible to lay them down succinctly in one chapter. The good news is that we will be exploring these topics within the Jarvin Media online community at two levels. The first is at the level of conceptual understanding. The second is at the 'so what' level. How does this understanding help me make sense of my experiences? And how does this understanding provide guidance for what I need to do to live my best life as a spiritual Being in a perpetual state of Abundance, Health, and Success? We hope that you will join us in this exploration.

And while there are some subtleties of the universe that are simply beyond our comprehension, acknowledging that we are all interconnected with everything in the universe is profoundly important for the way we live our lives. Our one job in life is to lift the veil of separation that descends upon incarnation and realize ourselves as an aspect of Source connected to 'all that is' in the universe.

CHAPTER 4

The Human Collective

The most profound realization that many people have when they embark on their spiritual journey is that we are all atoms of Source and eternal souls contained in energy having a myriad of incarnated experiences for the purpose of realizing ourselves as an aspect of Source.

This is profound because it helps us ponder our own life's purpose. Appreciating your life's purpose is one of the most vexing questions facing most of the 8 billion people living on this planet, let alone the endless number of other souls incarnated on the endless number of other lower worlds. This search for purpose is perhaps the one thing that binds us all as part of the human collective.

So, in this chapter, we will explore several topics related to the human collective that are offshoots of the central theme of 'the veil of separation' that exists within the lower worlds.

As Jen describes it, the lower worlds are those which operate within the confines of the physical, astral, causal, and mental planes of existence. These are the planes of existence at which the ego operates. The etheric plane is beyond the ego and is the gateway into the higher worlds. The higher worlds are well beyond the ego, and in which the veil of separation no longer exists.

The four planes of existence that represent the lower worlds operate at different vibratory rates. For example, the astral plane is so close in vibration to the physical plane that a lot of people find it difficult to perceive the difference between them. Yet they are different in energy. And the laws of physics that govern these planes are somewhat different.

For example, within the physical plane of existence, the laws of physics as we know them regulate the interaction and relationship between energy, matter, gravity, time, and space. On this plane of existence, we perceive time as linear, and we are bound by the laws of gravity. But on the astral plane, which is very close in energetic proximity to the physical plane, we can move more freely in time and space, and we are easily able to engage in astral travel beyond the confines of gravity.

The four planes of existence that define the lower worlds are very harsh in vibration relative to the higher worlds. When we incarnate into the lower worlds, we are bound by the limiting laws of physics that govern the lower worlds. These laws of physics create the veil of separation that descends upon us at the point of incarnation.

Jen often says that it is more difficult and traumatic to be born than it is to die. Upon death, the soul's consciousness is passed back to the astral body where it engages in a review process on the astral plane. This is what many new age spiritual practitioners describe as your 'life between lives', or 'the between life review process' with your spirit guides and soul group. Most people experience this as a pleasant and enlightening experience. It is free from the constraints of the physical realm. And for a period of time, you are plugged back into universal consciousness.

But for the most part, souls are programmed to be reborn to continue the process of expanding universal consciousness. Those who buy into the promise of 'heaven' as a place of eternal joy and happiness in the presence of God will find the concept of reincarnation particularly challenging.

Upon being reborn into the physical world, the soul is reintroduced to the laws of physics and limitations of the physical plane of existence. Part of the soul's consciousness is trapped within the mind of a new body and is separated from the collective consciousness. The veil of separation has once again descended. We can understand why this is a very lonely and traumatic experience for a lot of people, particularly those that describe themselves as starseeds.

Which begs an obvious question. Why on earth would anyone reincarnate into the lower worlds, with all the attendant constraints in doing so if they have the free choice not to? Why not just continue to exist in a non-corporeal form within the astral, causal, and mental realms? Or even better, why don't we just transcend the lower worlds altogether, pierce through the membrane of the etheric plane, and glide into the realms of the higher worlds?

Jen and Marvin have spent a lot of time exploring these intriguing questions. Is it the case that 'the Lords of Karma' keep us trapped within an endless cycle of reincarnation into the worlds of duality, pain, and suffering? Do we have free will at all with respect to reincarnation?

The answers to these questions lie within a simple notion. There is a dominant and almost overpowering force within the universe that seeks to expand consciousness. It is like the underlying driving force that perpetuates life on Earth. Or the force that drives salmon to run the gauntlet of migrating upstream to spawn new life.

Universal consciousness expands through experiences. Experiences are best had within the coarse vibration and duality of the lower worlds. So, as much as it may be traumatic and lonely to reincarnate into the lower worlds under the veil of separation, the drive to do so for the purpose of expanding universal consciousness is so dominant that we reincarnate out of habit. It is part of our nature as eternal souls. And we tend to keep doing so until we have had all possible experiences in the lower worlds such that there is nothing more to add to universal consciousness from our continued reincarnation. It is at this point that we transcend the ego and glide through the membrane of the etheric plane into the higher worlds.

One of the cool things about Jarvin Media is that we are teaching humanity the pathway to actively choose whether they want to reincarnate into the lower worlds or not. And that pathway is to transcend the ego and recognize yourself as omniscient, omnipresent, and omnipotent Beings. At this point, you have the awareness of your choice to reincarnate, and do not simply do it out of habit.

The veil of separation experienced by souls incarnating into the lower worlds is one of the things that unite us as part of the human collective. We are all on a journey to realize ourselves as an atom of Source seeking to return to Source and transcend the lower worlds. The difficulty is that there are several aspects of the human experience that perpetuate the separation from Source and the human collective.

As if it is not bad enough that we incarnate into the lower worlds under the veil of separation, there are some things about the human experience and conditioning that perpetuate that sense of separation – both from Source and from the human collective. And that sense of separation then perpetuates the role played by the ego, duality, pain, suffering, the abuse of power, the loss of empowerment, and being trapped in the daisy of death. All of these outcomes are still unfortunately a significant part of the human experience.

Perhaps the most significant regression in consciousness away from a connection to the human collective and Source occurred when the concept of 'one life' was introduced into several mainstream religious belief systems. Why did this occur? Perhaps doing so elevated the status of religious leaders as a conduit to Source and served as a mechanism to control and influence the faithful. But in any case, it resulted in a significant disruption to a sense of connection to the human collective and to Source.

A lot of the challenges we observe in the world today can only be resolved when a large proportion of the population regain their connection to the human collective and to Source, and in doing so, reclaim their empowerment as omniscient, omnipresent, and omnipotent Beings.

So how do we do this in a world that operates under the veil of separation, and in which greed, self-interest and indifference are so prevalent? One of the most profound things you can do is to change your vantage point from taking to outflowing. When you outflow, you give back to humanity, the Earth, and the universe.

So, folks, here is the thing. Your primary job as an incarnated soul is to transcend the ego as a pathway to lifting the veil of separation from the human collective and from Source. When thought about in these terms, a lot of people begin to question the importance and relevance of all of the things they have done in their life that have kept them busy but have distracted them their real purpose. So, here is your opportunity to get back onto the path to higher consciousness.

CHAPTER 5

Waking to Awakening

More and more people are awakening to the realization that their existence extends well beyond the physical world they observe on a day-to-day basis. They are beginning to realize that they are in fact spiritual Beings having a human experience for the purpose of expanding universal consciousness. They are beginning to realize that they are connected to Source and 'all that is' in the universe. They are beginning to realize that they have an energy body that operates simultaneously on five planes of existence. And many people are becoming highly attuned to perceiving in energy.

The primary purpose of life is to transcend the ego as part of the ascension process under the veil of separation that descends at the time of incarnation. Most souls have unsuccessfully struggled through this process over many thousands of lives. During most of those lifetimes, most of us have not even been aware of our primary purpose. Such is the heaviness of the veil of separation. We have bumbled through life after life in a state of ignorance, all the while accumulating experiences and collecting karma.

So, it is encouraging to observe that a lot of people are at least waking to the awakening process. The problem is that a lot of people get stuck on the first couple of rungs of the full spectrum of the spiritual journey. Awakening to yourself as a spiritual Being is just the first step. Then the real work begins. And there are plenty to traps along the way. In a lot of ways, the spiritual journey is like a game of 'slides and ladders', known in some parts of the world as 'snakes and ladders.' As you get more and more awareness, you diligently advance up the ladder. And then the ego kicks in and you slide down a couple of rungs of the ladder. Ah, the ego!

As we describe the rungs on the spiritual ladder, we will also lay out some of the traps so that you can avoid them as best as possible. But before we do, we should point out that as appealing as it is to lay out a spiritual journey in linear terms, it is not linear at all.

To begin with, there is no clearly defined boundary between one ladder rung and the next. There is no well-defined destination. And the revelations experienced on the lower rungs tend to be more earth shattering than those typically experienced on the higher rungs. At the lower rungs, these experiences come as wakeup calls that knock you out of complacency. So don't be too surprised that you get less of that sugar rush buzz as you advance in your spiritual journey.

The first rung on the spiritual ladder that we will describe is having that 'holy shit' awakening moment. It is that moment or instant when you suddenly realize you are an eternal spiritual Being connected to Source. Our sense is that most people who identify as being 'spiritual' have had at least one of these epiphany moments. They can come at various life stages and as a result of any number of stimuli.

Some people have near-death experiences that give them a brief glimpse of the 'other side'. It provides them with experiential evidence of life after death. A lot of people who have had a near death experience report a sense of being out of their body, seeing a tunnel of light, seeing and being in the presence of deceased loved ones, and having a sense of timelessness while they are having a life review.

What they are experiencing is what it is like on the astral plane during their life-between-lives. The astral plane is just another plane of existence that is not too far disconnected in energy from the physical plane. It is not the eternal heaven that is promoted in mainstream religion. For the most part, it is a staging ground that prepares souls for their next incarnation.

The thing is that all incarnated souls have astral plane life-between-lives experiences. The issue is that they then reincarnate under the veil of separation and do not have conscious recall of their past lives or their akashic record. A near-death experience is the physiological situation that allows those having the experience to actively navigate the astral plane. But people on a spiritual path are increasingly becoming more attune to perceiving in energy, reading akashic records, and having out of body experiences on the astral plane.

Near-death experiences are fascinating. And they get a lot of airtime within the spiritual and alternative reality community. But they are by no means the most prevalent catalyst for 'holy shit' moments. A lot of people have their 'holy shit' moment as a result of experiencing one or a number of life changing events that knock them out of the comfort of their previous existence. Examples of these include losing your job, getting a diagnosis, losing a loved one, being forced to relocate, or being uprooted by a cataclysmic force of nature. Typically, these kinds of life changing events force people to confront the 'why' question, which then gets answered in an instant – like being struck by lightning.

Still others have their 'holy shit' moment after going through years and years of dissatisfaction. You find yourself increasingly questioning and becoming dissatisfied with mainstream religion, authority, the nine-to-five of life, marriage, or community expectations. You feel empty and devoid of purpose or identity.

We like to think of this as the boiling frog effect. In this scenario, the pressure of dissatisfaction builds up slowly over time until the conditions are met, often at the most unexpected moment, for you to stumble across some kind of 'alternative truth' that resonates with you. What is funny about this scenario is that it is exactly this kind of 'alternative truth' that you would have previously rejected as being either foo-foo or just plain ridiculous. Our intention is that the dissatisfied diaspora will somehow and magically find this book, and that this book will be the catalyst of their 'holy shit' awakening moment.

The second rung on the spiritual ladder is the process of searching for and trying to make sense of truth. Those on this rung will learn about reincarnation possibly for the first time in their life. They will be confronted with the notion of karma. They will discover chakras. They may try yoga, meditation, and chanting. Later, they will probably sign up for a third eye opening workshop or dabble with ayahuasca. Hell, they might even read and get lost in the writing of Eckhart Tolle!

This rung is probably the most euphoric in terms of stimulating the pleasure principle. But it is also the most challenging rung to navigate through. This is because the second rung contains the most traps. They come in three broad categories: buying too much into other people's bullshit, getting caught up in your own bullshit, and not being able to let go of the broader built-in bullshit. You see, it's all about wading through the bullshit.

There is a lot of truth out there in the spiritual community. For the most part, there is a high degree of consistency between the core messages provided by a range of spiritual teachers. But outside of these core themes of universal truth, there are a lot of ideas and practices that knock seekers out of their own empowerment and their ability to experience themselves as omniscient, omnipresent, and omnipotent Beings.

The big daddy in the 'other people's bullshit' category is becoming a devotee of a particular spiritual teacher, guru, or social media influencer that promises a short-cut path to enlightenment. As appealing as it is in this attention deficit social media driven landscape, the simple fact of the matter is that there is no such thing as a ten-step plan to enlightenment. And in any case, the spiritual path is a journey, not a destination. Too much attention is given to becoming enlightened as the last step on the spiritual path. While enlightenment is an important milestone, it is by no means the end of the journey. If anything, the real work begins after you have become enlightened.

Another way that some people get trapped in 'other people's bullshit' is by excessively seeking the guidance of alien Beings or other spirit guides. There is nothing wrong with getting guidance from higher consciousness. We do it ourselves all of the time. Jen regularly communes with the Adepts. But the trap is sprung when you give over your sovereignty to an authoritative source outside of yourself like Jesus or Archangel Michael. The trick is to access higher consciousness without disempowering yourself. The more you can access higher consciousness yourself rather than by channeling a 'higher' Being, the better. And in any case, who is to say that what you think is guidance from Archangel Michael is not just the wisdom of your higher self that you are tapping into?

Our favorite in the 'other people's bullshit' category is getting caught up in the latest fad of practices designed to give you the illusion of omniscience. Some examples of these include practices designed to getting yourself out of your body, meditating on the blue pearl, receiving shakti pat, activating your kundalini, tantric love-making, and opening your third eye.

There are three ways that these trendy practices disempower you. The first is thinking that you have to do these things in order to be spiritual. This is not true. The second is that many people that try these practices do not achieve the desired outcome and therefore feel like a failure. And thirdly, even if you do have esoteric experiences while doing these things, they tend to be transitory, illusory, and they 100 percent play on the pleasure principle. Deliberately stoking the pleasure principle in these ways is probably the quickest way of getting caught in the ego.

The ego is front and center in the 'believing your own bullshit' category. And almost everyone on the spiritual path falls into this trap at some time or other. You see, the eye-opening nature of the first tranche of truth received is so mind blowing that most people fixate on it and think they are Eddie the Expert in it. And they want to tell everyone else about it. They become the new age version of a missionary whose job it is to convert all others to their newfound truth. That is why there is so much noise out there on social media.

Sharing truth is important. But it is all about how that truth is delivered. It has to be done in an egoless state and without it being embellished with your own spin (aka, bullshit). Living that truth so that others see it firsthand is better. The highest form of living truth is to constantly outflow in ways that serve and uplift all of humanity.

The 'broader built-in bullshit' is probably the hardest to overcome. In a lot of ways, overcoming this trap is only realistically possible when you are well and truly down the spiritual journey towards experiencing yourself as an omniscient, omnipresent, and omnipotent Being. The 'broader built-in bullshit' is the illusion of the physical laws that we buy into when we incarnate into the lower worlds. These are the laws of physics as we know them that regulate the interaction and relationship between energy, matter, gravity, time, and space. On the physical plane, we perceive time as linear, and we are bound by the laws of gravity. But in the higher realms, there is no time and space. Energy and matter are just aspects of each other. And the laws of gravity do not limit the ability to be in all places in the moment. Everything exists in the moment.

Jen often describes us as being an emanation of light and a frequency of sound woven together in the illusion of form. In this sense, we are first and foremost energy. The trick for us having an incarnated human experience is to recognize ourselves as such. This is a really hard thing for most people to do. This is because most of us have very tangible experiences in the physical realm. To suggest that the physical world is an illusion seems absurd to many people.

The most practical way of overcoming the illusion of time and space is to be perpetually present in the moment. A lot of people lament the past or are anxious about the future. And while they do these things, they miss the opportunity to be grateful in the moment. So, stay in the moment. And if you find yourself being tortured by the past or the future, use the SFT tapping protocols to free yourself from their clutches. The great thing about the SFT tapping protocols is that they operate in all moments.

The third rung on the spiritual ladder is becoming aware of your own ego. Understanding the ego and productively working with it is quite a challenge for a lot of people. We have seen many people who are quite spiritually aware, but who are still very much hostage to their own ego. The way this is manifested is in attitudes and behaviors that put the self over others. Taking rather than giving. Demanding rather than surrendering. Championing your own empowerment and sovereignty without affording it to all others. Being closeted in your own opinions rather than being open to all vantage points.

The fourth rung on the spiritual ladder is transcending the ego. The process of transcending the ego is called ascension or enlightenment. It is a process, and it is described in detail in the next chapter. While enlightenment is all about transcending the ego, that does not mean that enlightened people do not have an ego. As long as you retain physical form in the lower worlds, you need the ego. But enlightened people know how to work with the ego in a productive and healthy manner.

There is a misconception within the spiritual community that enlightenment is the holy grail end of the spiritual journey. It is not. There is also a strong misconception as to what an enlightened soul looks like. A common image of an enlightened soul is a guru perpetually meditating in the mountains, such as in the image below.

This notion is well past its 'use by date'. More and more ascended masters are living and operating in the 'real' world, in local communities, and in plain sight. And while they are enlightened, they still face real (if not unique) challenges in living and operating within the harsh vibration of the lower worlds.

So then, let's get to the fifth rung on the spiritual path. More accurately, this is the perpetual fifth rung. It does not end. It is the never-ending journey of being enlightened, operating in an almost egoless state, perpetually outflowing, being omniscient, omnipresent, and omnipotent without the limitations of time and space, and yet retaining physical form. Perhaps the most challenging aspect of this is to experience yourself as an energy Being while also being present in the physical body at the same time.

Increasingly, those that operate within the fifth rung of the spiritual journey dedicate themselves to the upliftment of all souls in the lower worlds. But even highly evolved souls having an incarnated experience need some healing from time to time.

Jen is a prolific writer and a poet. One of Jen's early poems was called *Healers Reunite* published in Jen's book *Jenuine Poetry for Life: Poems to Uplift Humanity*.

That poem, and a number of others from Jen's poetry book, has been put to music by Kind Bud on his album *Jenuine Kind Bud: Songs to Uplift Humanity Inspired by the Poems of Jen Ward*. Here are the lyrics.

Healers Reunite

An echo fills the ancient sky
There's heard one universal cry
Percussions, movement, a rhythmic blend
Hands that heal, bodies mend.

The dance to capture visions lost
Regain freedom at all cost
Broken lives we all endure
Remembering wholeness is the cure.

To wash away the ills of Man
Unite us with our tribe again
In this life few understand
What the Shaman can withstand.

To ease the suffering of those she can
Heart to heart and hand to hand
Eons later old friends dispersed
To meet as strangers is the curse.

Ways of remembering now dull and gray
All searching for the easy way
The healer steps forward in the artificial light
To show the brilliance of true sight.

Ancestors dance with spirits of earth and wind
Enhance the process of remembering
All seekers of truth squint to see
The humble stance of the Shaman's decree.

She summons the spirits, blows away the pain
Calls love back to the earth again
Folds time and space to make things right.
With the bending of pure light.

Others break through to the night
Remembering their vows to reunite
As coaches and healers they regather their clan
Inspired to mend the broken land.

We meet again across time and space
See recognition in a weary face
Fellow healers endured at all costs
And thought many times that all was lost.

Feel the blessings that do ensue
When one who awakens learns there's two
Exponential healing has begun
Spiritual freedom is now rewon!

CHAPTER 6

Ascension Realized

We have previously touched on the idea that the purpose of life is to outflow and expand universal consciousness through your experiences in a series of incarnated lives. We have also touched on the drive to transcend the ego as an opportunity to slip through the membrane of the etheric plane and therefore gain access to the higher worlds.

What we are really talking about here is the process of ascension. Ascension is another word for enlightenment, the achievement of which is a primary objective for many people within the spiritual community. Some spiritual paths adopt the idea that enlightenment is the holy grail, which once attained puts you at the lofty heights of gurus, saints, and siddhas.

It is certainly the case that enlightened souls and ascended masters are to be treasured. But becoming enlightened is not the end goal by any stretch of the imagination, especially when you still retain a physical presence as an incarnated Being. Once you become enlightened, your real work as a teacher, guide, and healer starts to take over your more mundane struggles of existing and merely surviving within the coarse vibration of the lower worlds.

Earth and humanity are at a tipping point. There is a real risk that the human experiment will come to an end if a critical mass of people on the planet do not ascend now. This is why there are so many spiritual teachers, spirit guides, advanced beings, and Adepts working tirelessly with humanity to assist in this mass ascension process. They are all doing their part. So, it would behoove us all to pay attention and do the work required for our own ascension.

Mainstream religion and societal norms teach us to be good. But in a lot of ways, focusing on being good denies us the opportunity to recognize the aspects of ourselves that are not good. Part of the purpose of life as a spiritual Being having a human experience is to have all experiences of duality within your repertoire – both positive and negative. Old souls will have had many thousands of incarnated lives within the lower worlds. In more than a few of them, you will have been both the perpetrator and the victim of truly horrible scenarios. So, none of us are as pure as the driven snow.

Enlightenment is a formulaic process. It is all about looking at yourself in totality. You will be pushed to the brink of insanity to recognize your own dark nature, and when pushing through it, you will realize that it is all an illusion. You will then enjoy three days of bliss in an egoless state. At the end of those three days, the ego rejoins the soul. This is because the ego is required to survive within the lower worlds. But from that time on, the soul is always keeping the ego in check to make sure it does not run amok again.

Enlightened souls have sufficient awareness and connection to the macrocosm that they are no longer driven to habitually reincarnate. They have had all the experiences they need to accumulate in the lower worlds, and they have transcended the ego. However, it seems that many ascended masters choose to reincarnate into the lower worlds for the purpose of assisting humanity in the mass ascension process. Others it seems, outflow and assist humanity in an energy body and not in a corporeal form.

Going through the process of enlightenment requires being pushed to the edge of insanity. That was certainly true in Jen's case.

She had left her ordinary life to move in with a sociopath in a state in America which was home to neither of them. They weren't romantically involved. But because of her lack of intimate relationships and feelings of unworthiness, she agreed to be with someone who was obsessed with aliens, well-versed in alternate realities, and psychically acute.

Jen was suddenly isolated from all she knew. She was sensory deprived from the restrictions he put on her. She was able to access all his insanity as if it were her own. On top of that, he went from being kind to her, to accusing her of stealing his abilities. He became paranoid of her and started accusing her of being the enemy.

She was alienated even more by being told she was the cause of all of the suffering in the world. A lot of negative personas were accredited to her, like Darth Vader, Jack the Ripper, and even Satan. She was constantly berated, sleep deprived, and constantly reminded of how bad she was.

She was forced to drink glass after glass of vinegar water to flush out the negativity in her. She was also forced to take high doses of niacin which caused a violent reaction in her body, turning it beet red with excruciating hives and leathery skin. In this state, the sociopath would make her look in the mirror and see herself as Satan himself.

Her sense of Self became drastically skewed. When she closed her eyes, she would see horrific imagery from the viewpoint of depravity. A common one was being an old man chained to a wall amongst a million other prison cells. He was emaciated and naked except for a rotted loincloth. There was a hole in the rugged rock wall that poured a paste of sewage into his reach. His only means of sustenance was to eat it. The world above him was clueless or indifferent to the misery of millions like him.

A few scenarios of depravity would play through Jen's mind that pushed her to the edge of insanity. For example, an evil genius created lab specimens to generate energy. One was a biologically generated rat that was a living ball of many rats combined in one. It had many legs and many heads, each of which was trying to run in its own direction. This inner conflict was a means to collect energy to be fed on. The same laboratory kept an innocent little girl perched alone in a dark cage. This was another means of feeding off the goodness of others.

There were regular scenarios of debauchery that repeated themselves at quicker intervals. There was a weird burlesque show with one man wearing only a boa entertaining in a club by stimulating himself as he danced and ejaculating on the audience. There were horrific monsters of the 1950's horror flicks entering a dungeon room with a beautiful woman and ravaging her in rape. There was a cave where the creations of a mad genius existed.

Within all the ugly imagery were the first drawings of Disney characters in their rudimentary form. They were eerily frightening in their contrast with the other scenes. They were just another means of feeding on people's energy through drawings of cute sympathetic characters. Jen would see the formulation of their early drawings dancing in a lab. She didn't understand the significance of this until much later. It was using the innocence of people to draw them into willingly giving up their energy to their own demise. The world is being destroyed by big business. Yet people continue to agree with their existence to feed some small creature comfort. It is like their imagination itself is being harvested and distorted and used to control humanity.

The neighbors, who the sociopath thought were members of the illuminati, seemed to take a special interest in Jen. They would only show up when Jen was pushed to the wall and trying to leave. Then there was a grandmotherly woman who started inviting them over for picnics. The head of house would come over when Jen wasn't working hard enough and encourage the sociopath to work her harder.

She cleared a lot of brushes, stumps, and trees in the hundred-degree Fahrenheit heat to seemingly extract the last bit of stamina from her. All the brush that she cleared out from acres of land was collected into a huge brush pile that was bigger than two or three houses next to each other. This pile stayed in the back yard until the neighbors felt it was safe to burn.

The night Jen went through enlightenment was maddening for her. The sociopath was telling her that she was the evil in the world that needed to be destroyed. She and he went from saving the world together, to her being the one that they were saving the world from. This set her mind in a loop of denial, justification and finally succumbing to this reality. It pushed her through the 'eye of the needle'.

When she looked at the wall, the shadowy images of debauchery became more and more alive. They started to dance on the wall and pull her in. She was drawn at warped speed through a tunnel of different experiences. For her, it felt like going through rooms at an alarming speed with a thin sheet separating each room from the last. It was her zooming through all of her lifetimes at warped speed and landing in a new realm.

The cave she got used to visiting in her dreams was now gutted of all its debauchery. It was an empty cavern where the sun now pierced through. Everything was cleansed by the light. The mad scientist's laboratory was gone. All the inventions and creations of the selfish mind were gone. Even the prison cell containing the old man in the loin cloth was empty and the door was open. She was walking in a clean cavern.

She was drawn outside to overlook a beautiful world. The cave always seemed like it was underground. But now it was at a high altitude overlooking the world. She observed a courtyard below. There was the Disney princess Cinderella and her prince dancing in a beautiful spring scenery. The seasons changed right before her eyes as they danced. She was being shown an understanding beyond time. She was controlling the change of seasons with her mind.

Her attention was drawn to the sky. There was a planet being formed like a soap bubble being formed through a wand. Then there was another, and another, and another. She then knew that she was creating these planets with her imagination and her intentions. She wondered whether they would be peaceful and loving planets or ones of war and discord. This was her being taught the ramifications of her thoughts and responsibility to always create planets of substance and integrity with her intentions.

She was then pulled back into the body with alarming speed. In the corner of the room was a huge tubular membrane from ceiling to floor that took up a huge section of the room. It emitted a sickening rhythmic sound that was the antithesis of joy. It sounded a lot like the chant of the scary monkeys in the Wizard of Oz movie. It was a throbbing pulsing rhythmic vortex of power. It was difficult for her to be so close to it. She was physically nauseous and disoriented.

She continued to lay in place and try to orient herself. But when she opened her eyes, a shadow appeared on the wall of an orgy scene. First it was an outline like hand shadows. Then it started to dance in place and became filled with detail. As soon as she focused on it, she was pulled out of her body from within and taken on another excursion. This kept happening as she tried to stay present in her body. She kept being sucked out of her body through the dancing image of the orgy on the wall.

She started to cry. She admitted to the sociopath how awful she was and all the things she had done and all the imagery she was seeing. She was surprised when he had compassion for her and talked nicely to her. This helped her to relax. It was then that she realized she was different. All the jealousy and pettiness that was being triggered in her was gone. All the self-consciousness and scrutiny were gone. She was at peace. This was apparent to the sociopath as well. She got to sit up for the first time in days.

As nighttime fell, there was a validation that something had shifted. The huge pile of brush that she had collected since she arrived on the property was being lit on fire by the neighbor. It was a huge blaze in the night sky. It was somehow an exhilarating expansiveness of freedom. It was also a form of validation to Jen that this experience she was having was a collaboration and it was important to the world. At this stage, she had no great sense of her healing abilities or her contribution to humanity through her writings and SFT tapping protocols. But for some reason, her going through this experience was important in the greater scope of life.

Jen was able to be outside for three days. She experienced the purity of an egoless state. The sweet resolve and peace she felt were a contrast to the racing and strategizing of the average mind. She thought this peace was her new natural state. The sound abomination in the corner was fading. She could still be easily pulled out of her body through the imagination. But it became more controllable. Her senses were still very heightened and acute. But then she got a sense of an unsettling 'presence' returning to her.

She thought it was an evil overtaking her because of the coarseness of its vibration. But it was just the ego being returned to her. She was told inwardly that the ego is a necessary mechanism for protection while in the physical world. What we call enlightenment is the ego getting pulled out and cleansed while the physical, emotional, causal, and mental bodies are realigned. Then the ego is returned to the body.

The ego assists us in staying present in the physical body and allows us to navigate the reality of the lower worlds while also being aware of the vastness of the universe we are actually a part of. The veil between this world and the others is monitored by the ego. It only allows information through that is deemed helpful to one's physical existence. All the striving and seeking up until the point of enlightenment is trying to convince the ego that truth is relevant to your physical life.

People think that enlightenment will give them a great advantage over others. But it took Jen a few more months to get out of the living situation that she was in. This egoless state that was now part of her makeup was described by the sociopath as being like a retarded boy.

It took Jen almost ten years to process this experience as being the process of enlightenment. And as dynamic as it might seem to the reader, it was simply Jen's own personal story of survival. Jen is convinced that everyone's own experience is much more satisfying than knowing of hers. But if it helps people tap into their own enlightenment, then she is happy to share.

Jen went through this horrific process so that others can access the experience of enlightenment without having to go through the terrifying experience alone. Perhaps all the insanity in the world is people all over the world being pulled through the process of enlightenment themselves and feeling terrified at the natural isolation of it.

Perhaps it will benefit others to understand that this experience of their own private hell has a purpose and a completion. Perhaps realizing that others are passing through it as well is important. Ascension is a formulaic process of being forced to look at all of the aspects of humanity that reside within us, accepting them as an aspect of ourselves, and pushing past the illusion of their reality.

CHAPTER 7

Nature's Wisdom

The natural world is in constant and perfect balance with the ebb and flow of energy within the universe. It takes in and absorbs energy in one form, uses it for its own purpose, and then gives it back in another form so that the broader ecosystem can survive and thrive.

We are often awestruck by the harmony and balance of all living things and matter within the universe. We sometimes wonder how this perfect complex system evolved. Was it by intelligent design? Or was it because of some natural evolutionary process? We tend to gravitate towards the latter as being the most likely.

There is something fundamental within the DNA of the universe that drives it to evolve and expand in consciousness. This DNA is often loosely described as sacred geometry. Sacred geometric patterns exist all around us. They are the perfect shapes and patterns that form the fundamental templates for life in the universe.

One form of sacred geometry is the Fibonacci sequence and the associated Fibonacci spiral. The Fibonacci sequence is the series of numbers 0,1,1,2,3,5,8,13,21, etc. The next number in the sequence is formed by adding together the previous two numbers in the sequence. Simple right? The

Fibonacci spiral is constructed by plotting the Fibonacci series on a grid. It looks like the diagram below.

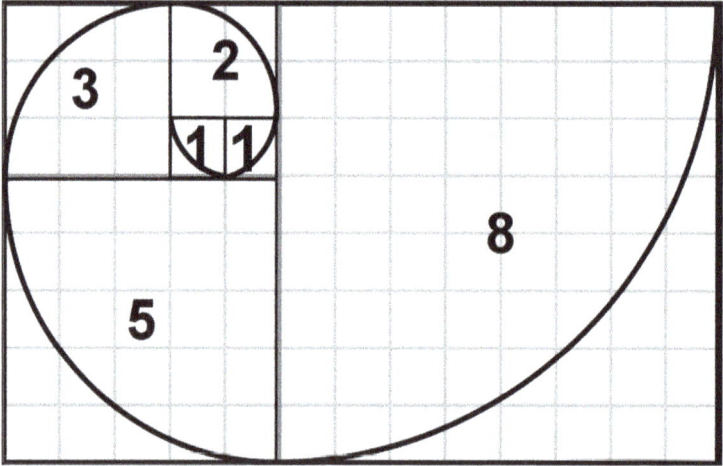

It turns out that the Fibonacci spiral is prevalent in nature. It is like it is the base code of universal structure and life itself. Examples of the Fibonacci spiral in nature are shown in the following collage of images.

Why is this important? Well, it shows that there is an underlying order within nature. All of nature is based on outflowing and expansion. It is intricately interconnected and balanced in the dance of energy. All animals perceive in energy as part of their sixth sense. Trees are connected to each other in energy through their root system. Birds collect and disperse stagnant energy as they fly.

So, it is interesting to note that humans are the one species on Earth that seem to be doing everything possible to control, harness, influence and subjugate the balance and harmony of the natural world.

Technology has allowed the human population to expand at an alarming rate. The extraction of fossil fuels and minerals has allowed us to produce all manner of goods and services for the excessive consumption pleasure of billions of people on the planet. But at what cost? All the pain, burden, limitations, disease, regret, and anxiety that people experience in the modern age is in large part the byproduct of being out of sync with nature.

And it gets worse. There are several people who are actively seeking to even further separate humanity from its natural environment by means of artificial intelligence. They promote the idea of dispensing with biological human systems altogether and propagating human consciousness throughout the universe in the form of self-replicating machines. Say what again?

Jen recalls in excruciating detail the anguish she experienced when reliving an engram of her consciousness being trapped in a cyborg body. She describes it as the loneliest experience possible. And she says that many people welcome pain in their present life because it is much better than the hollowness of having your consciousness eternally trapped in a cyborg body that has no feeling at all.

Our destiny is not to propagate human consciousness throughout the universe by means of machines and artificial intelligence. It is to expand in consciousness and to transcend the ego to the point where the soul can finally penetrate the membrane of the etheric plane and to therefore exist within the higher worlds.

Some people in Jen's private healing sessions are terrified of transcending the ego because they think that in doing so, they will be disconnected from their consciousness and identity. They think that existing in the higher worlds is like an existence of nothingness. We both feel that this is a misconstruction.

All that exists in the universe is programmed to outflow and expand in consciousness. Beings that exist in the higher worlds may no longer require a physical body. But that doesn't mean they exist in a state of nothingness. They outflow and expand universal consciousness through their interaction and guidance of Beings in the lower worlds to assist them in their journey towards transcendence.

It is vitally important that we disrupt the programming of those seeking to take humanity down a path of machine based artificial intelligence. One of the best ways to do this is for all of us to reconnect with nature, and to rejoin the natural evolution of souls in the natural world. Putting the effort into learning to communicate with nature is a great way to accelerate your ability to tap into your own divinity. Try doing some of these:

- Sit under a tree and ask to see the world from its vantage point.

- Read to a tree so that it can see the world from your vantage point.

- Have a conversation with a tree like it is your best friend.

- If you give a tree some of your spittle, it can read your energy to know what your needs are.

- Peeing under a tree is an intimate way of sharing with it, but perhaps not in public parks.

- Trees love to be sung to, so sing to your favorite tree. They will in turn inspire you to write your own songs. Many of the great song writers were downloading what the trees were giving them.

- Trees love to be validated. To listen to a tree is a way to get them to speak more with you. The more you listen, the more they will give you.

- Trees can tell you things it knows from its history. The older a tree is, the longer its resume of information that it can share with you.

- If you want to get into a creative moment, do the project under your tree and ask it for its help.

Of course, trees are not the only form of nature that you can reconnect with. Jen actively speaks to all forms of nature, both animate and inanimate. That is why she is so connected with her plushies.

Being in nature and communicating with nature is probably more important than you think. Nature is essential to ground and dissipate stagnant energy. It is like the way trees and other plant life absorb carbon dioxide and emit life giving oxygen. Nature captures stagnant energy and cleanses it. So, whenever possible, take the time to go to your local park. Instead of going on an overseas holiday, go on a hiking trip or overnight camping trip. And if you simply don't have access to nature, tune in to Jarvin Media and benefit from the nature videos that we create.

CHAPTER 8

Living a Spiritual Life

It is one thing to have the spiritual awareness and understanding contained within this book. It is entirely another thing to incorporate this understanding as a daily part of you living a spiritual life, becoming empowered, and experiencing perpetual Abundance, Health, and Success.

The overwhelming impression we get from the thousands of private healing sessions that Jen has done over the decades is that many people who are already on a spiritual journey are finding it tough going. We often wonder how people who are not on a spiritual path are coping. The purpose of this chapter, and indeed the entire book, is to give you context, hope and inspiration when traversing the seemingly chaotic dynamics of life.

It is useful to explore why so many people are finding it difficult to make sense of life these days. No doubt there are plenty of 'this world' contributing factors, including the pressure of the 24-hour news cycle, the impact of social media, the polarization of society, the increasing wealth gap, and the pressures and expectations that society puts on us in terms of careers, property ownership and family life. But we would like to explore this issue from a broader perspective.

There are two main things from a broader perspective that are contributing to the difficulties that a lot of people are facing when navigating through life. The first is the accelerated need to clear stagnant energy and engrams of past-life trauma to transcend the ego as part of the ascension process. The second is the increasing influence of intangible stimuli that a lot of people are struggling to process. It is the increasing and accelerated nature of these things that are causing a lot of people difficulty.

There is a real imperative to go through the ascension process at this time in Earth's evolution. Ascension is the process of transcending the ego. And as entrenched as it is, the ego is a fragile thing. It can be easily wounded. Confronting the ego can be a very painful process which brings forward emotions of anger, fear, loneliness, shame and regret. Little wonder then that a lot of people are bringing up painful emotions as we accelerate in the mass ascension process. Most people in the past have spent a lot of energy suppressing these emotions.

It is equally important to recognize that a lot of people are now beginning to experience energetic stimuli that they may not yet know how to process. These can come in the form of images, sounds, voices, or feelings. Having these new experiences 'out of the blue' can be very frightening and confusing. It could leave you feeling as if you are possessed or going insane. Several of Jen's private healing sessions are focused on helping clients navigate through these senses.

It is interesting to observe that a lot of people on the spiritual path are actively seeking to awaken their kundalini, receive shakti pat from a guru, or take ayahuasca to open their third eye. It seems to be trendy in the spiritual community to do these things. However, such instantaneous activations of energy, while exhilarating at the time, can be very challenging for a lot of people to process. It is preferrable to learn to walk before you run and go through the spiritual journey at a more natural pace. Remember, the biggest impediment to spiritual advancement is your ego.

There is no real step-by-step guidebook to living a spiritual life. That is why this is a short chapter. It is a journey, and it is unique to you. But we can offer some advice and insights to help you navigate through the seemingly chaotic dynamics of a spiritual life.

It is useful to understand that the challenging things you are experiencing are all part of the ascension process. It is formula. So simply having an awareness of what is going on will help allay a sense of isolation, confusion, and thinking you are losing your mind. You are not.

As difficult as it is in the moment, it is useful to look at situations and experiences from a detached or neutral position without labelling or judging them as either good or bad. There is something to be said about constantly living in a state of gratitude despite the day-to-day challenges. And most importantly, change your vantage point from taking to outflowing. You will be amazed at just how life-changing outflowing and service can be.

The Jarvin Media online community is a safe and inclusive place where you can directly interact with Jen and other community members. It is a major upgrade to posting on Facebook pages. And you can use the SFT tapping protocols to release yourself from in-the-moment issues and concerns.

CHAPTER 9

The SFT Tapping Protocols

While the ultimate purpose of life is to transcend the ego as part of a spiritual journey, most people, even the most spiritually aware, struggle to deal with real-world physical, emotional, psychological, and relationship issues. Most of these core issues stem from past-life trauma.

One simple and very tangible daily practice that everyone can do to release themselves from the clutches of past-life traumas and the ego is SFT tapping. Jen's SFT tapping protocols were developed by her over at least a decade with the guidance of the Adepts.

Jen has developed and refined four primary SFT tapping protocols that can be used to reclaim your energy from any person, issue, or situation. These include the *Energetic Cleanse*, the *Peanut Butter & Jelly Cleanse* (fondly referred to as the PB&J), the *Expunging Negativity Protocol*, and the *Positive Protocol*.

Make a list of all the things that disturb you and complete the SFT tapping protocols with each issue. Make sure you phrase the positive outcome you want to manifest in response to the issue when using the *Positive Protocol*. It will take you about an hour to complete the four protocols for each issue. So, if you are willing to invest an hour per day in your own ascension process, there are at least 365 issues that you can address per year. It is as simple as that.

SFT tapping and the four primary SFT tapping protocols developed by Jen are explained in detail in Jen's book, *The SFT Lexicon: Second Edition.* We encourage you to get your own copy of this textbook for life. But for your reference, here are the four primary SFT tapping protocols developed by Jen.

The Energetic Cleanse Protocol

Complete the entire protocol for a topic by saying each statement three times while continuously tapping on the top of your head, a fourth time while continuously tapping on your chest, and a fifth time while continuously tapping on your abdomen. Take a deep breath after finishing the series.

Feeling beholden to _____ is eliminated; in all moments.

All dependency on _____ is released; in all moments.

All claws of _____ are removed; in all moments.

All tentacles of _____ are removed; in all moments.

All vivaxes with _____ are removed; in all moments.

All glass ceilings that _____ have put on us are removed; in all moments.

The first cause of enabling _____ is eliminated; in all moments.

All curses with _____ are removed; in all moments.

All blessings with _____ are removed; in all moments.

All masks, walls and armor are removed from _____; in all moments.

All illusion is stripped from _____; in all moments.

All portals to _____ are collapsed and dissolved; in all moments.

All psychic energy of _____ is dissipated; in all moments.

All brainwashing or hypnotism of _____ is removed; in all moments.

All mind games of _____ are removed; in all moments.

All the pain, burden, limitations and engrams that _____ have put on us are removed; in all moments.

All the pain, burden, limitations and engrams that we have put on _____ are removed; in all moments.

All the pain, burden, limitations and engrams that we have put on others due to _____ are removed; in all moments.

All energy matrices that enable _____ are sent into the light and sound; in all moments.

All complex energy matrices that enable _____ are commanded into the light and sound; in all moments.

All contracts with _____ are nullified; in all moments.

All vows and agreements with _____ are recanted; in all moments.

All karmic ties with _____ are dissolved; in all moments.

All strings and cords with _____ are severed; in all moments.

All energy is withdrawn from _____; in all moments.

Resonating with _____ is released; in all moments.

Emanating with _____ is released; in all moments.

All that _____ has taken from us is returned; in all moments.

All that was taken from _____ is returned; in all moments.

All muscle memory of _____ is removed; in all moments.

All engrams of _____ are removed; in all moments.

All negative engrams that have been caused by _____ are removed; in all moments.

All of _____ is removed from our sound frequency; in all moments.

All of _____ is removed from our light emanation; in all moments.

All etheric echoes of _____ are removed; in all moments.

All etheric flecks of _____ are removed; in all moments.

Our paradigm is shifted from _____ to transcendence; in all moments.

All of _____ is transcended; in all moments.

The Wei Chi of all bodies is repaired; in all moments.

All bodies are aligned; in all moments.

We are centered and empowered in Divine Love; in all moments.

We resonate, emanate and are interconnected with all life in Divine Love; in all moments.

The Peanut Butter & Jelly Cleanse

Complete the entire protocol to separate the energy between X and Y by saying each statement three times while continuously tapping on the top of your head, a fourth time while continuously tapping on your chest, and a fifth time while continuously tapping on your abdomen. Take a deep breath after finishing the series.

All imbalances between _____ and _____ are released; in all moments.

All dysfunction between _____ and _____ is released; in all moments.

_____ being at the mercy of _____ is released; in all moments.

_____ being enslaved to _____ is released; in all moments.

_____ being the victim of _____ is released; in all moments.

All the suffering accrued between _____ and _____ is removed; in all moments.

All peripheral suffering caused by _____ and _____ is removed; in all moments.

_____ being manipulated by _____ is released; in all moments.

All injustice and inequality between _____ and _____ is removed; in all moments.

All exploiting and demigod interactions between _____ and _____ are released; in all moments.

All enabling between _____ and _____ is released; in all moments.

All blinders are removed from _____ or _____ in regard to one another; in all moments.

All agendas that _____ or _____ have put on the other are removed; in all moments.

_____ is free of the claws of _____; in all moments.

All tentacles between _____ and _____ are removed; in all moments.

All vivaxes between _____ and _____ are removed; in all moments.

All programming and conditioning between _____ and _____ is released; in all moments.

All negative engrams between _____ and
_____ are removed; in all moments.

All psychic energy between _____ and
_____ is dissipated; in all moments.

All brainwashing or hypnotism between _____ and
_____ is removed; in all moments.

All mind games between _____ and _____
are removed; in all moments.

All energy matrices are sent into the light and sound that
enable _____ or _____ to take from the
other; in all moments.

All complex energy matrices are commanded into the light
and sound that enable _____ or _____ to
take from the other; in all moments.

All masks, walls, and armor that _____ or
_____ have donned to protect one from the other are
removed; in all moments.

All contracts are nullified between _____ and
_____; in all moments.

All vows and agreements between _____ and
_____ are nullified; in all moments.

All curses between _____ and _____ are
removed; in all moments.

All blessings between _____ and _____ are
removed; in all moments.

All karmic ties between _____ and _____
are dissolved; in all moments.

All strings and cords between _____ and _____ are severed; in all moments.

All pain, burden and limitations between _____ and _____ are eliminated; in all moments.

All illusion of inadequacy, rejection, abandonment and separation between _____ and _____ is eliminated; in all moments.

All that _____ and _____ have taken from each other is returned; in all moments.

All resonating between _____ and _____ is released; in all moments.

All emanating between _____ and _____ is released; in all moments.

All need and dysfunction between _____ and _____ is removed from each other's Sound Frequency; in all moments.

All need and dysfunction between _____ and _____ is removed from each other's Light Emanation; in all moments.

All paradigms are shifted from the dysfunction of _____ and _____ to perpetual Joy, Love, Abundance, Freedom and Wholeness; in all moments.

All need and dysfunction between _____ and _____ is transcended; in all moments.

_____ and _____ are centered and empowered in perpetual Joy, Love, Abundance, Freedom and Wholeness; in all moments.

_____ and _____ resonate, emanate, and are interconnected with all life in perpetual Joy, Love, Abundance, Wholeness and Freedom; in all moments.

The Expunging Negativity Protocol

Complete the entire protocol for a topic by saying each statement three times while continuously tapping on the top of your head, a fourth time while continuously tapping on your chest, and a fifth time while continuously tapping on your abdomen. Take a deep breath after finishing the series.

All nefarious energies that cause _____ are unclenched from the microcosm, in all moments.

All nefarious energies that cause _____ are unclenched from the macrocosm; in all moments.

All nefarious energies that cause _____ are expunged from the physicality; in all moments.

All nefarious energies that cause _____ are expunged from the physical realm; in all moments.

All nefarious energies that cause _____ are expunged from the emotional make-up; in all moments.

All nefarious energies that cause _____ are expunged from the astral realm; in all moments.

All nefarious energies that cause _____ are expunged from all experiences; in all moments.

All nefarious energies that cause _____ are expunged from the causal realm; in all moments.

All nefarious energies that cause _____ are expunged from the mind; in all moments.

All nefarious energies that cause _____ are expunged from the mental realm; in all moments.

All nefarious energies that cause _____ are expunged from the belief system; in all moments.

All nefarious energies that cause _____ are expunged from the etheric realm; in all moments.

All disruptive energy matrices are sent into the light and sound that cause _____; in all moments.

All complex energy matrices are commanded into the light and sound that cause _____; in all moments.

The Positive Protocol

Complete the entire protocol for a topic you want to manifest by saying each statement three times while continuously tapping on the top of your head, a fourth time while continuously tapping on your chest, and a fifth time while continuously tapping on your abdomen. Take a deep breath after finishing the series.

Space is made in this world for _____ to manifest; in all moments.

All blockages to manifesting _____ are removed; in all moments.

All blockages to _____ are removed; in all moments.

All capacity to manifest _____ is stretched; in all moments.

All portals to manifesting _____ are opened; in all moments.

All walk through the portal to _____; in all moments.

The first and all subsequent causes to manifesting _____ are initiated and activated; in all moments.

All glass ceilings on manifesting _____ are removed; in all moments.

All portals that do not support _____ are collapsed and dissolved; in all moments.

The manifestation of _____ is infused into our Light Emanation and Sound Frequency; in all moments.

The manifestation of _____ is infused into the universal Light Emanation and Sound Frequency; in all moments.

All are centered and empowered in _____; in all moments.

All resonate, emanate, and are interconnected with all life in manifesting _____; in all moments.

Autocrats, Dictators, and Powermongers

Deplete the energy of autocrats, dictators, and powermongers by doing the following taps for yourself and as a surrogate for all of humanity. Say each statement three times while continuously tapping on the top of your head, a fourth time while continuously tapping on your chest, and a fifth time while continuously tapping on your abdomen. Take a deep breath after finishing the series.

1. We eliminate the first cause of enabling any and all maniacal individuals; in all moments.

2. We dissipate all psychic streams of energy that prop up any single individual as a God-Being on Earth; in all moments.

3. We strip all the self-importance off all those who professionally cause suffering in the world; in all moments.

4. We collapse and dissolve all power structures on Earth that create suffering and depravity; in all moments.

5.   We strip all illusion off all individuals who cause suffering and depravity in the world; in all moments.

6.   We gut the stockpile of energy that maniacal Beings have extracted from individuals as fuel, and return it to the collective; in all moments.

7.   We render all those who inflict suffering and depravity helpless and defeated; in all moments.

8.   We remove all masks, walls, and armor from all those who create suffering or depravity; in all moments.

9.   We close all portals in human history to any individual holding the collective hostage to their own selfishness and cruelty; in all moments.

10.   We send all energy matrices into the light and sound that enable any one individual to hold humanity hostage in suffering and depravity; in all moments.

11.   We command all complex energy matrices that enable any one individual to hold humanity hostage in depravity and suffering, to be escorted into the light and sound; in all moments.

12.   We release all engrams and muscle memory of all constructs of a male God; in all moments.

13.   We release all the programming and conditioning to worship a male God; in all moments.

14.   We release all transference of worshiping a male God to worshiping a maniacal human; in all moments.

15. We dissipate all psychic streams of energy that induce fear as a means of control; in all moments.

16. We release all engrams, muscle memory, constructs, and brainwashing that perpetuate primal mode; in all moments.

17. We free all individuals from the clutches of all those who cause suffering or depravity; in all moments.

18. We thwart all power structures and deactivate all armies that enable suffering and depravity; in all moments.

19. We immediately burst the bubble of all those who cause suffering or depravity; in all moments.

20. We deactivate all lifelines that enable those who cause suffering or depravity; in all moments.

21. We free humanity of the clutches of all those who cause suffering or depravity in the world; in all moments.

22. We dissipate all lines of communication and rhetoric that prop up anyone who causes depravity or suffering in the world; in all moments.

23. We knock all those who cause suffering or depravity in the world on their ass and out of the collective's energy system; in all moments.

24. We close all portals to all those who cause suffering or depravity in the world; in all moments.

25. We release all sense of false humility or unworthiness that is harnessed by powermongers; in all moments.

26. We release creating space in the world for those who cause suffering and depravity by deferring our empowerment; in all moments.

27. We release giving our empowerment by proxy to those who cause suffering and depravity in the world; in all moments.

28. We release playing it small so others can play big; in all moments.

29. We release the belief that we don't matter; in all moments.

30. We take back all the energy we have given to those who cause suffering and depravity; in all moments.

31. We repair and strengthen our energy field to address petty acts of power that we have enabled; in all moments.

32. We regain our voice; in all moments.

33. We regain our place at the center of the universe; in all moments.

34. We bow out of all hierarchy systems that enable suffering and depravity; in all moments.

35. We collapse and dissolve all hierarchies; in all moments.

36.   We release idolizing anyone; in all moments.

37.   We release diminishing anyone; in all moments.

38.   We release all sense of inferiority and superiority; in all moments.

39.   We defer from all pissing contests; in all moments.

40.   We collapse and dissolve the house of cards propping up anyone who causes suffering or depravity; in all moments.

41.   We release agreeing with anyone who advocates for suffering or depravity; in all moments.

42.   We eliminate the divide between the 'haves' and 'have nots'; in all moments.

43.   We dissipate all psychic streams of energy underlying the lies that powermongers tell; in all moments.

44.   We release deactivating our moral compass in regard to powermongers; in all moments.

45.   We release giving powermongers permission through our silence or apathy; in all moments.

Political Divisiveness

Take the sting out of political divisiveness by doing the following taps for yourself and as a surrogate for all of humanity. Say each statement three times while continuously tapping on the top of your head, a fourth time while continuously tapping on your chest, and a fifth time while continuously tapping on your abdomen. Take a deep breath after finishing the series.

46.　We release being perpetually trapped in an 'us versus them' mentality; in all moments.

47.　We release all division in the collective; in all moments.

48.　We release attacking the collective from within; in all moments.

49.　We release being a cancer cell on the wellbeing of the whole; in all moments.

50.　We extract all hypersensitivities to external differences; in all moments.

51. We release being triggered into reactionary mode by external differences; in all moments.

52. We thwart all attempts to divide the collective using outer differences as a response trigger; in all moments.

53. We remove all primal responses to perceiving differences as a threat; in all moments.

54. We release perceiving differences in others as a threat; in all moments.

55. We remove all engrams and muscle memory in all individuals that stoke tribalism through the differences in others; in all moments.

56. We remove all compartmentalization of humanity within a hierarchy of 'haves and have nots'; in all moments.

57. We remove all issues of entitlement or superiority from any subset of humanity; in all moments.

58. We remove all subtle forms of a caste system within the collective; in all moments.

59. We dissipate all psychic streams of energy that enslave subsets of the collective through infighting; in all moments.

60. We remove all engrams and muscle memory of a caste system from all individuals; in all moments.

61. We thwart all attempts to wield power by suppressing other subsets of the collective; in all moments.

62. We release the belief that any root race or other subset of the collective is superior to another; in all moments.

63. We release all belief systems and practices that demoralize subsets of humanity; in all moments.

64. We release all belief systems that invoke 'divine right' to abuse power; in all moments.

65. We collapse and dissolve all constructs that hold power through the notion of 'divine right'; in all moments.

66. We eliminate the first cause in stripping the power away from individuals; in all moments.

67. We thwart the hoarding of energy of political, religious, and business leaders; in all moments.

68. We give back to all individuals all the energy that was taken from them by political, religious, and business systems; in all moments.

69. We eliminate the first cause in turning on our brethren; in all moments.

70. We release infusing a reverence for God in our political system; in all moments.

71. We release the stoking of our passions to enliven political divisiveness; in all moments.

72.   We release the merging of religion with politics; in all moments.

73.   We release dehumanizing anyone who shows up as different to us; in all moments.

74.   We release being conditioned from birth to protect or defend a particular political ideology; in all moments.

75.   We release being driven to hate through the weaponization of social interactions; in all moments.

76.   We release the fervor to protect an ideology at all costs; in all moments.

77.   We release the drive to hate that is systemically stoked by social media; in all moments.

78.   We release being susceptible to all factions who work to weaponize individuals through ideology; in all moments.

79.   We dissipate all political campaigns and agendas that are a front for powermongers; in all moments.

80.   We strip all illusion off all attempts to weaponize an ideology; in all moments.

81.   We dissipate all psychic streams of energy that induce political division through primal fear; in all moments.

82.   We thwart the stoking of the psyche of individuals that causes political division; in all moments.

83.　We thwart the transfer of our reverence for God on political figures; in all moments.

84.　We extract all demigods and powermongers from the political system; in all moments.

85.　We strip all illusion off all powermongers and demigods that use politics as their altar; in all moments.

86.　We remove all masks, walls, and armor off all powermongers and those who wish to be elevated to demigod status; in all moments.

87.　We extract all hierarchy from all subsets of the collective that cause political division; in all moments.

88.　We remove all engrams and muscle memory from all individuals that cause them to be perpetually trapped in attack mode; in all moments.

89.　We remove all engrams and muscle memory from all individuals that cause them to be perpetually trapped in defense mode; in all moments.

90.　We release existing in the mentality that the enemy is everywhere; in all moments.

91.　We release elevating any ideology over kindness and compassion; in all moments.

92.　We free all individuals from the mind traps that keep them stuck in political division; in all moments.

The Drive to War

Eliminate the drive to war by doing the following taps for yourself and as a surrogate for all of humanity. Say each statement three times while continuously tapping on the top of your head, a fourth time while continuously tapping on your chest, and a fifth time while continuously tapping on your abdomen. Take a deep breath after finishing the series.

93.   We remove all souls from hell; in all moments.

94.   We remove all engrams and muscle memory of being at war; in all moments.

95.   We release all survivor's guilt from all those who have fought; in all moments.

96.   We release the glorification of war; in all moments.

97.   We release training our psyche to go to war through our entertainment venues; in all moments.

98.   We dissipate the constant barrage to kill through entertainment venues; in all moments.

99.   We release associating war with entertainment; in all moments.

100.   We strip all illusion off the reality of war; in all moments.

101.   We release associating war with glorifying death; in all moments.

102.   We extract all engrams and muscle memory of Viking lifetimes; in all moments.

103.   We release the belief that battle is spiritual; in all moments.

104.   We thwart all means of stoking our psyche to go to war; in all moments.

105.   We pull all individuals out of Valhalla; in all moments.

106.   We empty the halls of Valhalla; in all moments.

107.   We nullify all of Earth's soul contracts with war; in all moments.

108.   We release associating the surge of hormones in becoming an adult with the call to war; in all moments.

109.   We release confusing the drive to be considered an adult with the call to war; in all moments.

110.   We release the justification of an ethical war; in all moments.

111. We release being roused to war by magnetic personalities; in all moments.

112. We release being a pawn for power; in all moments.

113. We release all attempts to pull humanity into a holy war; in all moments.

114. We release the belief that any war is justified; in all moments.

115. We remove all platitudes in regard to war; in all moments.

116. We release all false equivalence between powermongers and those defending their sovereignty; in all moments.

117. We release confusing any conflict with the sacred intention of protecting one's sovereignty; in all moments.

118. We release being stoked to war through feelings of unworthiness; in all moments.

119. We release using going to war to feel important; in all moments.

120. We release going to war out of habit; in all moments.

121. We dissipate all psychic streams of energy that call us to war; in all moments.

122. We release going to war to settle a score from a past life; in all moments.

123. We dissipate all psychic streams of energy that call our children to war; in all moments.

124. We eliminate the first cause in being at war; in all moments.

125. We release the belief that war is inevitable; in all moments.

126. We remove ourselves from the river of hell; in all moments.

127. We release associating war with charismatic characters in movies; in all moments.

128. We thwart all creative ventures that profit from the glorification of war; in all moments.

129. We inspire all creative ventures to transcend the low hanging fruit of profiting through the glorification of war; in all moments.

130. We release driving our youth into the cul-de-sac of serving in the military; in all moments.

131. We release being charged with the fervor of war through competitive sports; in all moments.

132. We release using war as a means to an end; in all moments.

133. We release all boredom that drives us to war; in all moments.

134. We release confusing peace as a stagnant state of consciousness; in all moments.

135. We release using war to feel alive; in all moments.

136. We release going to war to get a sense of belonging; in all moments.

137. We release romanticizing war; in all moments.

138. We release using war to excite our senses; in all moments.

139. We release being driven to war out of loyalty, familiarity, or family legacy; in all moments.

140. We dissipate all psychic streams of energy of self-righteousness in going to war; in all moments.

141. We remove all programming of duty or honor in going to war; in all moments.

142. We release using war as a means to earn respect; in all moments.

143. We release going to war to over-compensate; in all moments.

144. We dissipate all psychic streams of energy of the proliferation of weapons; in all moments.

The Military
Industrial Complex

Break down the military industrial complex by doing the following taps for yourself and as a surrogate for all of humanity. Say each statement three times while continuously tapping on the top of your head, a fourth time while continuously tapping on your chest, and a fifth time while continuously tapping on your abdomen. Take a deep breath after finishing the series.

145. We release being used as a pawn for profit; in all moments.

146. We release allowing our morality to be dictated by those who profit from war; in all moments.

147. We remove all masks, walls, and armor off all those who profit from war; in all moments.

148. We collapse and dissolve all subcultures that benefit from the proliferation of the military; in all moments.

149. We release being used as a cog in the wheel of power; in all moments.

150. We question all authority that orders us not to question it; in all moments.

151. We release foregoing our sovereignty to those who profit off our agreement to serve; in all moments.

152. We release serving power; in all moments.

153. We release all indoctrination of power; in all moments.

154. We release being indoctrinated by the military; in all moments.

155. We release joining the military to get a sense of belonging; in all moments.

156. We release being trapped between a rock and a hard place in joining the military; in all moments.

157. We strip all illusion of self-righteousness from the military industrial complex; in all moments.

158. We release the stockpiling of power through the military industrial complex; in all moments.

159. We release the subjugation of humanity by superpowers; in all moments.

160. We shift the paradigm of the world from superpowers to universal empowerment; in all moments.

161. We thwart trapping individuals into serving in the military through constant fear-based threats; in all moments.

162. We release the belief that we are the superior faction; in all moments.

163. We remove all masks, walls, and armor off all military factions that feign innocence; in all moments.

164. We strip all illusion off all military factions that depict themselves as the victim; in all moments.

165. We release the foreboding doom and gloom that military leaders promote; in all moments.

166. We release the race to doomsday; in all moments.

167. We thwart all pissing contests by the military industrial complex; in all moments.

168. We disarm the military industrial complex of its favorite game of chicken; in all moments.

169. We remove all engrams and muscle memory of doomsday from Earth's akashic record; in all moments.

170. We reign in the military industrial complex; in all moments.

171. We remove all powermongers, sociopaths, and martyrs from the military industrial complex; in all moments.

172. We close all portals to humanity being a military state; in all moments.

173. We release the ability of power-hungry sociopaths to stand at the helm of the military industrial complex; in all moments.

174. We release the destruction of organic life by the military industrial complex; in all moments.

175. We release the desecration of humanity by the military industrial complex; in all moments.

176. We release worshiping the military industrial complex; in all moments.

177. We release the practice of allowing those in the military industrial complex to be beyond reproach; in all moments.

178. We collapse and dissolve the military industrial complex; in all moments.

179. We thwart all venues and timelines whose mainstay is suffering; in all moments.

180. We remove all lines drawn in the sand by military factions; in all moments.

181. We strip all glorified power out of the military industrial complex; in all moments.

182. We thwart overcompensating through the build-up of military stockpiles; in all moments.

183. We thwart all arms races to destruction; in all moments.

184. We release wasting our creative juices by creating bigger and better killing machines; in all moments.

185. We empty all power reserves from the military industrial complex; in all moments.

186. We release allowing the military industrial complex to move us further away from our humanity; in all moments.

187. We heal all the wounded little boys that use the build-up of power to try and comfort themselves; in all moments.

188. We knock all sociopaths and mass manipulators off the helm of the military industrial complex; in all moments.

189. We immediately and thoroughly thwart the weaponization of sound; in all moments.

190. We disarm the weaponization of sound; in all moments.

191. We transcend the perpetual pissing contest of the military industrial complex; in all moments.

192. We return individual and universal sovereignty to all Beings; in all moments.

Weapons of
Mass Destruction

Eliminate weapons of mass destruction by doing the following taps for yourself and as a surrogate for all of humanity. Say each statement three times while continuously tapping on the top of your head, a fourth time while continuously tapping on your chest, and a fifth time while continuously tapping on your abdomen. Take a deep breath after finishing the series.

193. We disarm all weapons of mass destruction; in all moments.

194. We release the scorched-earth mentality; in all moments.

195. We release reality imitating art; in all moments.

196. We release agreeing to a doomsday scenario; in all moments.

197. We release the belief that Earth is headed for a destructive cataclysm; in all moments.

198. We prevent all sociopaths and powermongers from holding the world hostage with nuclear weapons; in all moments.

199. We thwart all temper tantrums of sociopaths and powermongers; in all moments.

200. We close all portals to a scorched-earth scenario; in all moments.

201. We send all energy matrixes into the light and sound that draw Earth towards a doomsday scenario; in all moments.

202. We command all complex energy matrices that draw Earth towards a doomsday scenario to be escorted into the light and sound; in all moments.

203. We gut the stockpiling of weapons of mass destruction; in all moments.

204. We thwart the profiting off weapons of mass destruction; in all moments.

205. We thwart all attempts by autocrats and their power brokers to use weapons of mass destruction for personal gain or vendettas; in all moments.

206. We dissipate all psychic streams of energy that instigate temper tantrums using weapons of mass destruction; in all moments.

207. We eliminate the first cause in creating or using weapons of mass destruction; in all moments.

208. We release investing the creativity and imagination of humanity into builder better weapons of mass destruction; in all moments.

209. We release the belief that the use of weapons of mass destruction is inevitable; in all moments.

210. We remove the looming threat of weapons of mass destruction being used on humanity; in all moments.

211. We nullify all contracts between humanity and weapons of mass destruction; in all moments.

212. We erase the use of weapons of mass destruction from Earth's soul contract; in all moments.

213. We collapse and dissolve all trajectories where Earth is scorched by weapons of mass destruction; in all moments.

214. We return the empowerment of Earth to organic life and species; in all moments.

215. We release converting organic materials into weapons of mass destruction; in all moments.

216. We strip all illusion off all weapons of mass destruction; in all moments.

217. We immediately and thoroughly disarm all weapons of mass destruction; in all moments.

218. We rust out all the intentions to use weapons of mass destruction; in all moments.

219. We shift the Earth's paradigm from weapons of mass destruction to organic peace; in all moments.

220. We thwart all emboldening of powermongers through weapons of mass destruction; in all moments.

221. We remove the finger of powermongers from the button that initiates weapons of mass destruction; in all moments.

222. We release all the bravado of sociopathic powermongers based on their access to weapons of mass destruction; in all moments.

223. We release the glorification of weapons of mass destruction from our entertainment venues; in all moments.

224. We dissipate all thirst for the use of weapons of mass destructions by experiencing it in our entertainment venues; in all moments.

225. We release the compulsion to experience the traumatic use of weapons of mass destruction; in all moments.

226. We nullify all contracts, vows and agreements, with all weapons of mass destruction; in all moments.

227. We release the muffling of humanity's outcries regarding weapons of mass destruction; in all moments.

228. We release burying humanity in a tsunami of platitudes regarding weapons of mass destruction; in all moments.

229. We dissipate all psychic streams of energy of apathy regarding weapons of mass destruction; in all moments.

230. We release twisting the narrative that glorifies weapons of mass destruction; in all moments.

231. We thwart exemplifying mass empowerment using weapons of mass destruction; in all moments.

232. We extract all of humanity's integrity, strength, and honor from weapons of mass destruction; in all moments.

233. We thwart all attempts to use weapons of mass destruction as a pissing contest; in all moments.

234. We extract all the fear, potential suffering, and doomsday scenarios from the prospects of using weapons of mass destruction; in all moments.

235. We make whole all those who have been damaged by weapons of mass destruction; in all moments.

236. We heal all aspects of Earth that have been wounded by weapons of mass destruction; in all moments.

237. We thwart humans using power beyond their means of insight; in all moments.

238. We gift all humans with the propensity and capacity to disengage from valuing weapons of mass destruction; in all moments.

239. We thwart the worship of weapons of mass destruction; in all moments.

240. We repair all fractured DNA in all humans that cause them to tolerate the existence of weapons of mass destruction; in all moments.

241. We repair and fortify the Wei Chi of the Earth that was damaged through the use of weapons of mass destruction; in all moments.

Conspiracy Theories

Collapse disinformation and conspiracy theories by doing the following taps for yourself and as a surrogate for all of humanity. Say each statement three times while continuously tapping on the top of your head, a fourth time while continuously tapping on your chest, and a fifth time while continuously tapping on your abdomen. Take a deep breath after finishing the series.

242. We release searching for truth by indulging in conspiracy theories; in all moments.

243. We release all gullibility that causes us to believe in conspiracy theories; in all moments.

244. We strip all illusion off all conspiracy theories; in all moments.

245. We thwart the hard-wiring of conspiracy theories into our convictions; in all moments.

246. We remove the mystery and intrigue from conspiracy theories; in all moments.

247. We release searching for truth through lateral means; in all moments.

248. We release the need to believe in something outside of ourselves; in all moments.

249. We release giving up our own empowerment to conspiracy theories; in all moments.

250. We release giving up our balance to conspiracy theories; in all moments.

251. We release being distracted from truth through conspiracy theories; in all moments.

252. We release being trapped in the daisy of death by believing in conspiracy theories; in all moments.

253. We release undermining our own abilities to know truth by believing in conspiracy theories; in all moments.

254. We release weaponizing humans through their belief in conspiracy theories; in all moments.

255. We dissipate all psychic streams of energy that distract humans from their purpose using conspiracy theories; in all moments.

256. We release being trapped in the mental realms through conspiracy theories; in all moments.

257. We strip all illusion off all those who perpetuate conspiracy theories; in all moments.

258. We untangle all humans from the psychic twine of conspiracy theories; in all moments.

259. We release giving up our inner vision to outer circumstances promoted by conspiracy theories; in all moments.

260. We release putting our faith in conspiracy theories; in all moments.

261. We thwart all means of powermongers maintaining power through the use of conspiracy theories; in all moments.

262. We release the weaponization of humans using conspiracy theories; in all moments.

263. We release allowing conspiracy theories to distract us from rejecting a manmade God; in all moments.

264. We release investing our belief system in conspiracy theories; in all moments.

265. We separate all truths from the lies of conspiracy theories; in all moments.

266. We thwart the practice of mixing half-truths with many lies to control the masses; in all moments.

267. We strip all illusion off the originator of conspiracy theories; in all moments.

268. We remove all engrams and muscle memory that causes us to fall prey to conspiracy theories; in all moments.

269. We release confusing the natural state of awakening with the nefarious intentions of powermongers; in all moments.

270. We release the attack on common sense and the ability to reason in regard to conspiracy theories; in all moments.

271. We release confusing nefarious intentions with the splendor of tapping into higher truth; in all moments.

272. We release the belief that truth can be given to us from an outside source; in all moments.

273. We release using conspiracy theories as a means to deny ourselves access to our own akashic records; in all moments.

274. We give ourselves permission to remember and learn from our past lives; in all moments.

275. We release demonizing the practice of remembering our past lives; in all moments.

276. We release denying the truth that is blatantly within us and shows up in our dreams; in all moments.

277. We release thwarting our own truth by falling for conspiracy theories; in all moments.

278. We remove all engrams and muscle memory of being punished, tortured, or killed simply for accessing truth; in all moments.

279. We release using conspiracy theories to quench our thirst for truth; in all moments.

280. We release searching for a means to awaken using conspiracy theories instead of accessing our own truth; in all moments.

281. We release losing all confidence in our ability to know truth; in all moments.

282. We release needing our inner truths validated by an outside source; in all moments.

283. We release believing conspiracy theories instead of the wondrous truth we access within; in all moments.

284. We release all the bastardization of truth that conspiracy theories conjure up; in all moments.

285. We remove all masks, walls, and armor from all those who create conspiracy theories to accrue power; in all moments.

286. We give back to all humans all the energy they have invested in conspiracy theories; in all moments.

287. We remove the shackles of control that conspiracy theories have put on humanity; in all moments.

Secret Agendas

Implode secret world governments and other secret agendas by doing the following taps for yourself and as a surrogate for all of humanity. Say each statement three times while continuously tapping on the top of your head, a fourth time while continuously tapping on your chest, and a fifth time while continuously tapping on your abdomen. Take a deep breath after finishing the series.

288. We release being controlled through our sacred beliefs; in all moments.

289. We release worshipping a man-made concept of Source; in all moments.

290. We release the primal need to belong; in all moments.

291. We release giving away our power in a myriad of ways; in all moments.

292. We release being conditioned by social niceties; in all moments.

293. We remove all muscle memory and engrams that were instilled in us through secret agendas; in all moments.

294. We strip all illusion off all secret agendas; in all moments.

295. We remove all masks, walls, and armor from all secret agendas; in all moments.

296. We release being born into a cesspool of hidden agendas; in all moments.

297. We release being controlled by secret agendas; in all moments.

298. We release being knocked off balance as the illusion of hidden agendas is stripped away from us; in all moments.

299. We release the fear of having the truth of hidden agendas stripped away; in all moments.

300. We release being a pawn to hidden agendas; in all moments.

301. We release the damage we have inadvertently done to others due to our loyalty to hidden agendas; in all moments.

302. We release being manipulated by secret agendas that stoke our fears; in all moments.

303. We release the stoking of parts of our brain that keep us in step with secret agendas; in all moments.

304. We repair the amygdala of our brain; in all moments.

305. We release being contained in primal mode through secret agendas; in all moments.

306. We dissipate all psychic streams of energy that embolden secret agendas; in all moments.

307. We thwart the normalization of secret agendas and their control as our mainstay; in all moments.

308. We release sabotaging our own awakening by falling into the trap of yet another secret agenda; in all moments.

309. We release the belief that secret agendas are necessary or noble; in all moments.

310. We release the desecration of noble intentions that mutate into secret agendas; in all moments.

311. We release all aversion and fear of taking the red pill; in all moments.

312. We release the propensity to choose the blue pill; in all moments.

313. We release the fear of the consequences of rejecting all secret agendas; in all moments.

314. We remove all engrams and muscle memory of being ostracized that cause us to comply with secret agendas; in all moments.

315. We release being emotionally blackmailed by secret agendas; in all moments.

316. We release being watched by the controlling eye; in all moments.

317. We untangle our passion for truth from the nefarious tentacles of secret agendas; in all moments.

318. We release confusing power factions with a means to connect to Source; in all moments.

319. We release all beliefs that cause us to cling dearly to secret agendas; in all moments.

320. We remove the grip of secret agendas from our beingness; in all moments.

321. We release making allowances for our pet secret agenda; in all moments.

322. We nullify all contracts with all secret agendas; in all moments.

323. We remove all vivaxes with all secret agendas; in all moments.

324. We recant all vows and agreements with all secret agendas; in all moments.

325. We strip all illusion off the secret agendas that we have fallen prey to; in all moments.

326. We release being trapped in the worlds of illusion through secret agendas; in all moments.

327. We remove all curses and limitations that secret agendas have put on us; in all moments.

328. We transcend all secret agendas; in all moments.

329. We withdraw all our allegiance and energy from all secret agendas; in all moments.

330. We free all those that we have offered up to secret agendas; in all moments.

331. We remove all the pain, burden, and limitations that secret agendas have put on us and those we have offered up to them; in all moments.

332. We remove all engrams and muscle memory of being offered up, martyred or sacrificed to secret agendas; in all moments.

333. We release serving power through our agreement with secret agendas; in all moments.

334. We free all of humanity from the throws of secret agendas; in all moments.

335. All of humanity transcends secret agendas; in all moments.

336. All of humanity releases resonating or emanating with secret agendas; in all moments.

337. All of humanity shifts its paradigm from serving power to embracing love through self-empowerment; in all moments.

Extremism and Hate Fueled Violence

Temper extremism and hate-fueled violence by doing the following taps for yourself and as a surrogate for all of humanity. Say each statement three times while continuously tapping on the top of your head, a fourth time while continuously tapping on your chest, and a fifth time while continuously tapping on your abdomen. Take a deep breath after finishing the series.

338. We release all self-righteous anger; in all moments.

339. We dissipate all psychic streams of energy that fuel hate; in all moments.

340. We strip all illusion of superiority or self-importance from all humans; in all moments.

341. We remove all engrams and muscle memory that stoke hate; in all moments.

342. We release pulling past-life grievances into the present; in all moments.

343. We release being hard-wired to hate; in all moments.

344. We release being stoked to violence through our choices for entertainment; in all moments.

345. We release stroking the fervor of violence in society; in all moments.

346. We release the belief that violence is the answer; in all moments.

347. We remove all engrams and muscle memory of the fervor for battle; in all moments.

348. We release confusing the fervor for conflict with masculinity; in all moments.

349. We release using violence to overcompensate for shortcomings; in all moments.

350. We remove the collective from the primal mode of being driven to violence; in all moments.

351. We thwart the myriad of ways that humans are stoked to violence; in all moments.

352. We release humanity pissing away the energy reserves earmarked for awakening through being driven to violence; in all moments.

353. We release the petulance and immaturity ingrained in the human condition that drives them to violence; in all moments.

354. We release using violence to deflect from self-accountability; in all moments.

355. We release plummeting to the depth of despair through the compulsion of hate-fueled violence; in all moments.

356. We remove all engrams and muscle memory of hate from our akashic records; in all moments.

357. We release the stoking of hate through charged imagery and symbols; in all moments.

358. We disarm all imagery and symbols that invoke violence; in all moments.

359. We release forfeiting our sovereignty to fuel hate; in all moments.

360. We recant all vows and agreements of revenge; in all moments.

361. We extract all hate-induced blood oaths; in all moments.

362. We release glorifying hate or violence; in all moments.

363. We release the justifying of hate and violence; in all moments.

364. We release inducing ourselves and others to hate; in all moments.

365. We release likening hate to a sugar rush; in all moments.

366. We release poisoning the pool with hate and violence; in all moments.

367. We release confusing hate and violence with spirituality; in all moments.

368. We release being trapped in the dead-end of hate-fueled violence; in all moments.

369. We thwart all compulsion to snowball into hate-fueled violence; in all moments.

370. We eliminate the first cause of fueling violence with hate; in all moments.

371. We release depleting our kundalini energy in the activation of hate; in all moments.

372. We release being poisoned by hate; in all moments.

373. We release being so easily stoked to hate-fueled violence; in all moments.

374. We release operating from the low vibration of hate; in all moments.

375. We release being a carrier of hate; in all moments.

376. We release amusing ourselves with hate-fueled violence; in all moments.

377. We release the sugar rush of conquering others; in all moments.

378. We release being indifferent to the residual byproduct of suffering that hate-fueled violence induces; in all moments.

379. We release being susceptible to manipulation and control by easily being driven to hate-fueled violence; in all moments.

380. We release forming a sense of belonging in bonding with others who are susceptible to hate-fueled violence; in all moments.

381. We release foregoing our ability to reason; in all moments.

382. We release lowering our vantage point and vibration through commiserating in hate-fueled violence; in all moments.

383. We release agreeing to add our energy to fuel hate driven violence; in all moments.

384. We convert all the vibration of hate to the vibration of empowerment; in all moments.

385. We deactivate the primal urge to digress to violence; in all moments.

386. We release bullshitting ourselves that hate-fueled violence is an option; in all moments.

Inequality and Injustice

Remove inequality and injustice by doing the following taps for yourself and as a surrogate for all of humanity. Say each statement three times while continuously tapping on the top of your head, a fourth time while continuously tapping on your chest, and a fifth time while continuously tapping on your abdomen. Take a deep breath after finishing the series.

387. We remove all engrams and muscle memory of individual and universal slavery; in all moments.

388. We disrupt the dance between being the conqueror or the slave; in all moments.

389. We dissipate all psychic streams of energy that embolden the dance of the conqueror and enslavement; in all moments.

390. We remove the hard-wiring of humans to accept the dance of the conqueror and the slave; in all moments.

391. We refute the programming and conditioning in religious texts that normalizes conquering and enslavement; in all moments.

392. We remove the agreement within humanity to be either the conqueror or the slave; in all moments.

393. We release playing out the dynamics of the conqueror and the slave in the collective; in all moments.

394. We free all individuals and all of the collective from swinging between the polarities of the conqueror and the slave; in all moments.

395. We free all subsets of the collective from playing the part of either the conqueror or the slave; in all moments.

396. We nullify all contracts between all subsets of the collective to actively participate in being either the conqueror or the slave; in all moments.

397. We release playing out the dance of the conqueror and the slave within society; in all moments.

398. We release the propensity to gravitate to the role of either the conqueror or the slave; in all moments.

399. We remove the dance of the conqueror and the slave within all governing and religious systems; in all moments.

400. We release being conquered by any governing or religious factions; in all moments.

401. We release the playing out of the dance between the conqueror and the slave within families; in all moments.

402. We release being hard-wired to be the conqueror; in all moments.

403. We release being hard-wired to be enslaved; in all moments.

404. We release forgetting all the spiritual lessons of being either the conqueror or slave that we have accrued through a multitude of lifetimes; in all moments.

405. We release the trauma of being forced to be either the conqueror or the slave; in all moments.

406. We release having our spark of empowerment taken from us from all the lifetimes of being the conqueror or the slave; in all moments.

407. We release being broken into an existence of being either the conqueror or the slave; in all moments.

408. We remove all vortexes between all conquerors and slaves; in all moments.

409. We nullify all contracts with all conquerors and slaves; in all moments.

410. We remove all the pain, burden, and limitations that all conquerors and slaves have put on each other; in all moments.

411. We eliminate the first cause in the dance of the conqueror and the slave; in all moments.

412. We give back to all conquerors and slaves all that the other has taken from them; in all moments.

413. We collapse and dissolve all archaic energetic exchange systems between the conqueror and the slave; in all moments.

414. We remove all of the sociopathic God-complex mentality from all those hard-wired to conquer; in all moments.

415. We remove all the systemic unworthy martyrdom mentality hard-wired in those who gravitate towards being a slave; in all moments.

416. We remove all programming and conditioning within families, religions, governing, learning, and socio-economical systems that reinforce the dance between the conqueror and the slave; in all moments.

417. We calm the psyche of all conquerors and afford them the freedom to lay down their sword and shield; in all moments.

418. We repair the energy field of all slaves and infuse them with all that they have been deprived; in all moments.

419. We erase the dance between the conqueror and the slave from all individual soul contracts; in all moments.

420. We release all Beings from their agreement to be a conqueror or a slave; in all moments.

421. We extract all of conquering and slavery from all individual's sound frequency and light emanation; in all moments.

422. We release all individuals from resonating or emanating with either conquering or slavery; in all moments.

423. We free all subsets of the collective and the Earth itself from resonating or emanating with conquering or slavery; in all moments.

424. All humans transcend the dance of conquering and slavery; in all moments.

425. All of nature and all species of life are freed of playing the slave to humans' compulsion to conquer; in all moments.

426. All humans are stripped of the illusion of their superiority in regard to nature and other species; in all moments.

427. All subsets of the collective and humanity itself transcends the dance of conquering and slavery; in all moments.

428. All humans and all aspects of the collective are centered and empowered in their organic empowerment; in all moments.

429. All humans and all aspects of the collective resonate, emanate, and are interconnected with all life in their organic empowerment; in all moments.

Poverty and Hunger

End poverty and hunger by doing the following taps for yourself and as a surrogate for all of humanity. Say each statement three times while continuously tapping on the top of your head, a fourth time while continuously tapping on your chest, and a fifth time while continuously tapping on your abdomen. Take a deep breath after finishing the series.

430. We release the disparagement and void between the 'haves and have nots'; in all moments.

431. We release all entitlement that creates poverty and hunger in the world; in all moments.

432. We remove all engrams and muscle memory of starving; in all moments.

433. We release all engrams and muscle memory of devastating lack; in all moments.

434. We release causing lack and hunger through being driven to excess; in all moments.

435. We release the disconnect in the collective between the 'haves and have nots'; in all moments.

436. We release being driven to excess through our innate understanding of lack; in all moments.

437. We shift the paradigm of all individuals from poverty and hunger to perpetually having enough; in all moments.

438. We remove all engrams and muscle memories that stoke us to hoard; in all moments.

439. We thwart the sucking up of all the oxygen in the room; in all moments.

440. We release propagating on a level that creates systemic poverty and hunger; in all moments.

441. We release depleting our universal resources; in all moments.

442. We remove all shortsightedness that perpetuates poverty and hunger; in all moments.

443. We release the apathetic overindulgence in greed; in all moments.

444. We gift all humans with the propensity to understand the lack they create through their everyday choices; in all moments.

445. We release the disconnect in humans between their choices and their ability to affect universal empowerment; in all moments.

446. We remove all blockages to universal empowerment; in all moments.

447. We thwart all the hoarding of other's providence; in all moments.

448. We gut the stockpile of abundance that powermongers have taken from individuals and convert it back into individual sovereignty; in all moments.

449. We eliminate the first cause in raping the providence of all individuals in the collective; in all moments.

450. We free the 'have nots' from being enslaved to the entitled; in all moments.

451. We collapse and dissolve the hierarchies that maintain the disparagement between those in lack and the entitled; in all moments.

452. We release the raping of humanity's creativity, imagination, and empowerment; in all moments.

453. We raise the vibration of the 'have nots' to personal empowerment; in all moments.

454. We soften the vibration of the entitled to the vibration of compassion and kindness; in all moments.

455. We gift all those who are entitled with the ability to see the results of their indifference; in all moments.

456. We clear the pathway of all those in poverty and hunger to owning their empowerment; in all moments.

457. We thwart all individuals from vacillating between entitlement and lack within the span of their lifetimes; in all moments.

458. We remove the veil of ignorance that prevents individuals from realizing their empowerment; in all moments.

459. We release the compulsion for more; in all moments.

460. We release associating accruing more with the primal experience of hunting and gathering; in all moments.

461. We release associating a stockpile of more with the primal scnsc of security; in all moments.

462. We thwart the stoking of our primal urge to accrue more; in all moments.

463. We thwart the over profiting from human consumption through rampant commercialism; in all moments.

464. We collapse and dissolve the trillion-dollar industry that programs and conditions individuals to consume to excess; in all moments.

465. We dissipate the psychic streams of energy that prompt individuals to create waste through buying what they don't need; in all moments.

466. We shift the paradigm of all takers from influx to outflow; in all moments.

467. We shift the paradigm of all those in need from the vibration of lack to the vibration of satiation; in all moments.

468. We extract the vibration of want and need from the collective; in all moments.

469. We remove the collective from the primal dance between entitled hoarding and lack; in all moments.

470. We afford all individuals the propensity to transcend both lack and entitled hoarding; in all moments.

471. We remove all programming and conditioning of false humility that traps individuals in poverty and hunger; in all moments.

472. We release the belief that Source wants us to suffer; in all moments.

473. We release the belief that it is more spiritual to be in lack or to starve; in all moments.

474. We release martyring ourselves to sects of the collective through different forms of lack; in all moments.

475. We remove all programming and conditioning that God loves us for our lack; in all moments.

476. We release starving the collective of love and compassion; in all moments.

477. We dry up all poverty and hunger; in all moments.

478. We spread the wealth of empowerment evenly around the world; in all moments.

479. We thwart all opportunists from profiting in any way off creating poverty or lack in the world; in all moments.

Overpopulation

End the propensity of humans to procreate out of habit by doing the following taps for yourself and as a surrogate for all of humanity. Say each statement three times while continuously tapping on the top of your head, a fourth time while continuously tapping on your chest, and a fifth time while continuously tapping on your abdomen. Take a deep breath after finishing the series.

480. We release procreating out of habit; in all moments.

481. We release being emotionally blackmailed to procreate; in all moments.

482. We release being psychically bribed to procreate; in all moments.

483. We release destroying the planet with our compulsion to procreate; in all moments.

484. We dissipate all psychic streams of energy that compel us to procreate; in all moments.

485. We release being breeders for profiteers; in all moments.

486. We release being enslaved to parenthood; in all moments.

487. We collapse and dissolve all constructs that mandate procreation; in all moments.

488. We release being programmed and conditioned to breed; in all moments.

489. We remove all engrams and muscle memory of procreating; in all moments.

490. We release romanticizing parenthood; in all moments.

491. We release the systemic practice of forgoing one's purpose to procreate; in all moments.

492. We remove ourselves from the treadmill of procreating out of habit; in all moments.

493. We remove the primal fear from the collective that it will be abandoned in its old age if the population dwindles in numbers; in all moments.

494. We release all shortsightedness in the relationship between overpopulation and natural resources; in all moments.

495. We release treating Earth with a throw away mentality by using up its resources through over-procreating; in all moments.

496. We release procreating for selfish wants; in all moments.

497. We release procreating out of ignorance; in all moments.

498. We release the total lack of responsibility to others in over-procreating; in all moments.

499. We release the belief that God wants us to go forth and multiply; in all moments.

500. We remove all curses that man-made God proclamations have put on humanity; in all moments.

501. We release phasing out all other forms of life due to over-procreating; in all moments.

502. We release waiting for the universal force of natural selection to kick in to thin the herd; in all moments.

503. Humanity naturally thins the herd through conscientious procreating instead of through cataclysm; in all moments.

504. Earth avoids looming towards disaster through overpopulation; in all moments.

505. We release the belief that procreating for the sake of procreating is a spiritual or noble cause; in all moments.

506. We release procreating to overcompensate for inadequacies; in all moments.

507. We release the bullshit mentality that having children for the sake of having children is sacred; in all moments.

508. We release shaming those who bow out of procreating; in all moments.

509. We release the plague of overpopulation from the earth through the gentle means of thoughtful procreation; in all moments.

510. We release romanticizing big families; in all moments.

511. We remove all engrams and muscle memory of the security and sanctity of big families; in all moments.

512. We release the pestilence mentality in regard to procreating; in all moments.

513. We release reducing the quality of life for all through the quantity of humans coming through; in all moments.

514. We release depleting Earth's natural resources through the compulsion to procreate; in all moments.

515. We release elevating parenthood to a more noble purpose than other forms of purpose; in all moments.

516. We release being trapped in the primal mode that causes humans to procreate out of habit and fear; in all moments.

517. We remove all blockages to only the awakened incarnating; in al moments.

518. We release the onslaught of ignorance of incarnating through habitual procreation; in all moments.

519. We remove all blockages to supporting higher understanding and awareness regarding procreation; in all moments.

520. We collapse and dissolve all governing mandates that force procreation on the populace; in all moments.

521. We immediately and thoroughly thwart all attempts to limit freedom by forcing woman to procreate; in all moments.

522. We strip all illusion off the bullshit control that a fetus is a sovereign Being; in all moments.

523. We release choosing quantity of life over quality of life; in all moments.

524. We release elevating the concept of a baby to a demigod position; in all moments.

525. We strip all illusion off the mentality of procreating; in all moments.

526. We immediately and thoroughly thwart the ability of religions and governing bodies to mandate procreation to keep their numbers up; in all moments.

527. We knock all humans out of primal mode in regard to procreating; in all moments.

528. We remove the "elephant in the room' of religious and political factions using the abortion issue to control the narrative; in all moments.

529. We release the practice of distracting humans through taking a 'them vs us' stance on procreation; in all moments.

530. We strip all illusion off all those who use the notion of procreation to profit or accrue personal power; in all moments.

531. We strip all illusion, masks, walls, or armor off all profiteers of the baby-making industry; in all moments.

532. We release all passion for procreation that is fueled by nefarious intentions of profiteers and powermongers; in all moments.

533. We immediately transcend the self-slavery mentality of altruistic procreating; in all moments.

534. We release martyring ourselves, humanity, and Earth to an outmoded mentality and understanding of procreating; in all moments.

535. We release agreeing to ignorance through our personal choices; in all moments.

536. We release sentencing Earth to mass slavery through our personal choices and limited understanding; in all moments.

537. We release revering the fetus over those who are presently incarnated; in all moments.

538. We immediately forgo the 'one life' understanding that creates a moral issue where there is none; in all moments.

539. We release forcing a fetus to incarnate into unfavorable situations to appease the misplaced moral outrage of the uninformed; in all moments.

540. We remove all blockages to all individuals having access to their akashic records; in all moments.

541. We release stripping a fetus of its right to choose by forcing it to incarnate; in all moments.

542. We transcend the melodrama of subjugating women through interfering with their procreation decisions; in all moments.

543. We remove all male entitlement in regard to a woman's procreation choices; in all moments.

Disease

Address core issues that cause disease by doing the following taps for yourself and as a surrogate for all of humanity. Say each statement three times while continuously tapping on the top of your head, a fourth time while continuously tapping on your chest, and a fifth time while continuously tapping on your abdomen. Take a deep breath after finishing the series.

544. We release making space for cancer at the table by talking about it; in all moments.

545. We release elevating cancer and disease to an acceptable part of the human experience; in all moments.

546. We release rallying around cancer; in all moments.

547. We release celebrating cancer by default through celebrating cancer survivors; in all moments.

548. We dissipate all psychic streams of energy that elevate cancer through attaching it to our loved ones who have survived; in all moments.

549. We dissipate all psychic streams of energy that connect the color of our precious baby girls with the life and death struggle to survive cancer; in all moments.

550. We release all the subtle ways that cancer has infiltrated our society; in all moments.

551. We release inadvertently celebrating cancer through pink ribbons, fund raisers, and romanticizing the fight of survivors; in all moments.

552. We release forfeiting our sovereignty through emotional issues that show up as physical issues; in all moments.

553. We release the disconnect between emotional issues and physical disease; in all moments.

554. We release the disconnect between past-life issues and present diagnoses; in all moments.

555. We release carrying the consciousness of being a victim in a past life to being a victim in the present life through the manifestation of a disease; in all moments.

556. We release getting on the treadmill of disease by avoiding self-responsibility regarding health issues; in all moments.

557. We release going into fear and victim consciousness when developing symptoms; in all moments.

558. We remove the curse of the word 'terminal' from the human analogues; in all moments.

559. We release giving our power to a third party in regard to our health and choices; in all moments.

560. We remove all the ways we curse our health; in all moments.

561. We remove all negative dialogue and programming from our repertoire; in all moments.

562. We release all fear and aversion to addressing a health issue; in all moments.

563. We release resonating with the disease of someone we are close to as a form of love; in all moments.

564. We extract all genetic propensity for disease from our DNA; in all moments.

565. We release all forgone conclusions in regard to a diagnosis; in all moments.

566. We release being at the mercy of profiteers in regard to our health; in all moments.

567. We dissipate all psychic streams of energy and all programming and conditioning that affects our health in any way; in all moments.

568. We release being bombarded and manipulated in making unhealthy choices for our body; in all moments.

569. We remove all blockages to healthy choices related to self-care; in all moments.

570. We thwart the global practice of putting profit over person in the healthcare system; in all moments.

571. We release choosing disease through a martyr mentality; in all moments.

572. We release using disease as an escape from responsibility; in all moments.

573. We remove all blockages to avoiding disease; in all moments.

574. We remove all internal struggles regarding our health; in all moments.

575. We release being paralyzed in fear when dealing with health issues; in all moments.

576. We release the 'them versus us' mentality between western medicine and alternative practices; in all moments.

577. We remove all curses on our health by other people's filters in regard to an issue; in all moments.

578. We release inadvertently creating health issues as emotional blackmail; in all moments.

579. We release indulging in negative scenarios in regard to health issues; in all moments.

580. We release invoking cancer or other issues into our world by saying the word; in all moments.

581. We release entertaining ourselves with disease through gossip; in all moments.

582. We release desecrating the personal pursuit of health by talking about it to others; in all moments.

583. We sever all strings and chords between ourselves and any word, manifestation, or vibration of disease; in all moments.

584. We release our body from confusing the doctor, scalpel, or any other implement of healing as an enemy with a weapon; in all moments.

585. We remove all cells of our Beingness from primal fear; in all moments.

586. We remove all blockages to listening to our gut or heart in regard to health issues; in all moments.

587. We release the belief that a diagnosis automatically looms us towards death; in all moments.

588. We release the belief that death is inevitable in regard to disease; in all moments.

589. We release the belief that God is testing us or punishing us in regard to disease; in all moments.

590. We release indulging in doomsday trajectories in regard to disease; in all moments.

591. We release indulging the dramatic display of the ego in regard to disease; in all moments.

592. We extract all issues from all our physical, emotional, causal, and mental body that weigh us down with disease; in all moments.

593. We extract all issues from every cell of our essence; in all moments.

Environmental Catastrophe

Avoid environmental catastrophe by doing the following taps for yourself and as a surrogate for all of humanity. Say each statement three times while continuously tapping on the top of your head, a fourth time while continuously tapping on your chest, and a fifth time while continuously tapping on your abdomen. Take a deep breath after finishing the series.

594. We thwart all profiting through the rape of Earth; in all moments.

595. We immediately eradicate the creating and use of forever chemicals; in all moments.

596. We release the shortsightedness of poisoning ourselves through the proliferation of forever chemicals; in all moments.

597. We release the mentality of moral high ground or any justification in using forever chemicals; in all moments.

598. We break down all forever chemicals to natural organic substances; in all moments.

599. We release the desecration of earth and the genocide of life through forever chemicals; in all moments.

600. We release unleashing the mentality of genocide on the planet and into our earth, air and waterways through forever chemicals; in all moments.

601. We interrupt the disconnect between cancer and forever chemicals; in all moments.

602. We release sacrificing humans to profiteers through the use of forever chemicals; in all moments.

603. We eliminate the first cause and all subsequent causes in unleashing forever chemicals on the planet; in all moments.

604. We release the phasing out of organic life and the human existence through poisoning the planet with forever chemicals; in all moments.

605. We remove all portals to AI being the only existence that can survive on the planet due to the proliferation of forever chemicals; in all moments.

606. We strip all illusion, masks and armor off of all profiteers that use forever chemicals to succeed; in all moments.

607. We shift the paradigm from using forever chemicals out of convenience to finding an organic means to problem solve; in all moments.

608. We release putting profit over quality of life; in all moments.

609. We thwart the ability of profiteers to initiate causes that negatively affect the whole; in all moments.

610. We afford all humans with the foresight and ability to know the consequences of putting out their intentions; in all moments.

611. We remove all disconnect between cause and effect; in all moments.

612. We repair the connection between cause and affect and the ability of humans to see it; in all moments.

613. We free humans from the immaturity to expect someone else to undo their nefarious intentions; in all moments.

614. We reinstate integrity, accountability and self-responsibility to all humans and all subsets of the collective; in all moments.

615. We release creating cataclysmic disasters through our desecration of Earth; in all moments.

616. We release all the ways in which we desecrate Earth; in all moments.

617. We release treating Earth like something we can use up and through away; in all moments.

618. We dissipate all psychic streams of energy that cause humans to use up the natural resources of Earth at an alarming rate; in all moments.

619. We release the ignorance and arrogance of man that believes he can deplete Earth and move on to another planet; in all moments.

620. We release the apathy, ignorance, and denial that prevents humans from taking responsibility for their overconsumption of Earth's resources; in all moments.

621. We release the practice of billionaire profiteers holding humanity hostage through the compulsion to accrue more wealth for themselves; in all moments.

622. We strip all illusion off all nefarious intentions and profiteers that hold humanity hostage to their agenda; in all moments.

623. We dissipate all psychic streams of energy that invoke God or the bible to hold humanity hostage to profiteers; in all moments.

624. We immediately and thoroughly strip all illusion off all narratives that lead to the destruction of Earth; in all moments.

625. We disarm all billionaires from destroying Earth through their selfish nefarious intentions; in all moments.

626. We remove all curses on the fate of Earth; in all moments.

627. We remove all our energy from the destruction of Earth; in all moments.

628. We release being gutted of our organic connection to Earth; in all moments.

629. We release ignoring the cries of Earth and all its inhabitants; in all moments.

630. We remove all blockages to reconnecting with our organic nature; in all moments.

631. We release selling our soul and our fate to selfish profiteers; in all moments.

632. We extract all of Earth's energy from selfish profiteers and return it to Earth's organic nature; in all moments.

633. We release the split in trajectories between the narrative implanted in the collectives psyche by profiteers, and the intention for mass awakening; in all moments.

634. We send all energy matrices into the light and sound that perpetuate the destruction of Earth through the nefarious intentions of profiteers; in all moments.

635. We command all complex energy matrices that perpetuate the destruction of Earth to be escorted into the light and sound; in all moments.

636. We release invoking the teachings of any religious scripture to continue to enslave humanity in a destructive trajectory for Earth; in all moments.

637. We dissipate all psychic streams of energy that perpetuate humanity into looming catastrophe; in all moments.

638. We remove all curses on Earth regarding catastrophic outcomes; in all moments.

639. We close all portals to earth being an unlivable environment; in all moments.

640. We release replacing organic life with artificial instruments; in all moments.

641. We send all energy matrices into the light and sound that enable catastrophic scenarios on Earth; in all moments.

642. We command all complex energy matrices that enable catastrophic scenarios on Earth to be escorted into the light and sound; in all moments.

643. We transcend all scenarios that diminish the perpetual capacity and splendor of Earth; in all moments.

644. We thwart the proliferation of humans at an alarming rate; in all moments.

645. We thwart the proliferation of humans as a plague on Earth; in all moments.

646. We release the belief in humans that God wants them to procreate at all costs; in all moments.

647. We release elevating the life of humans over the right of other species to exist; in all moments.

648. We release sacrificing other species for the selfishness, and arrogance of humans; in all moments.

649. We thwart humans incarnating out of habit; in all moments.

650. We release allowing takers to incarnate on the planet; in all moments.

651. We remove all blockages to only the awakened incarnating if they chose to; in all moments.

652. We make space in the world for all trees to have sovereignty and even citizenship; in all moments.

653. We release the insanity of ignoring climate change; in all moments.

654. We immediately and thoroughly thwart looming towards uninhabitable conditions on Earth at an alarming rate; in all moments.

655. We release all blockages to the healing sounds of nature returning Earth to balance; in all moments.

656. We immediately and thoroughly eradicate all trajectories that lead to the destruction of humanity and Earth; in all moments.

Earth as an Ashcan

Remove the belief that Earth is the dumping ground of the universe by doing the following taps for yourself and as a surrogate for all of humanity. Say each statement three times while continuously tapping on the top of your head, a fourth time while continuously tapping on your chest, and a fifth time while continuously tapping on your abdomen. Take a deep breath after finishing the series.

657. We release the belief that Earth is the ashcan of the universe; in all moments.

658. We remove all curses on Earth; in all moments.

659. We release resenting Earth; in all moments.

660. We release the feeling that Earth is not our home planet; in all moments.

661. We release treating Earth as a throwaway planet; in all moments.

662. We release waiting for a superior alien race to come and save us; in all moments.

663. We release Earth from all its contracts of slavery; in all moments.

664. We remove the harshest vibrations from Earth; in all moments.

665. We remove the shroud of ignorance that envelopes Earth; in all moments.

666. We thwart all practices that seal Earth's fate as the ash can of the universe; in all moments.

667. We release Earth from being a way station for interstellar mercenaries; in all moments.

668. We release the corralling of humans in disempowerment through limiting belief systems; in all moments.

669. We release the fracturing of human DNA to keep them in darkness; in all moments.

670. We thwart all attempts to keep humans in ignorance by perpetually stoking primal fear in them; in all moments.

671. We release the propensity to keep Earth enslaved by preventing the awakening of humans; in all moments.

672. We merge all the trajectories of Earth into the most optimal version of itself in joy, love, abundance, freedom and wholeness; in all moments.

673. We close all portals to Earth being enslaved; in all moments.

674. We release all isolation of Earth from benevolent alien races; in all moments.

675. We raise the vibration of the planet through universal empowerment; in all moments.

676. We free Earth from being a penal colony; in all moments.

677. We remove all blockages to Earth perceiving assistance from benevolent alien races; in all moments.

678. We release being viewed as a rogue planet by alien races; in all moments.

679. We remove all blockages to being respected as equals by alien races; in all moments.

680. We release being kept in the dark ages regarding our relationship with other planets; in all moments.

681. We release being held in a systemic state of ignorance and apathy; in all moments.

682. We release reflecting limitations on our planet through our tendency to opt out of responsibility; in all moments.

683. We release being viewed as a throw away planet by species from other planets; in all moments.

684. We release being ignorant of other races of planets that don't operate in our limited band of reality; in all moments.

685. We remove all blockages to being aware of life on other planets; in all moments.

686. We release the barbaric mentality of intending to conquer and plunder other planets; in all moments.

687. We free earth from being enslaved to profiteers on other planets; in all moments.

688. We release being held in slavery by the notions of a controlling God; in all moments.

689. We remove all limitations that all other species from other planets have put on us; in all moments.

690. We release the centrifugal tendencies of Earth; in all moments.

691. We flush out all the dross from Earth; in all moments

692. We raise the vibration of Earth so life on other planets can interact with us; in all moments.

693. We transcend fear and primal mode so that life on other planets can reach out to us; in all moments.

694. We remove all engrams and muscle memory of warring tendencies from Earth; in all moments.

695. We release perceiving ourselves and Earth as victims; in all moments.

696. We relieve ourselves of a 'them versus us' mentality in regard to other planetary systems; in all moments.

697. We remove all blockages to communicating with other planets of varying vibratory rates; in all moments.

698. We release the fear of being abducted by aliens; in all moments.

699. We release perceiving ourselves as lab rats for other species; in all moments.

700. We make space in this world to know what we presently are not capable of knowing; in all moments.

701. We release sensationalizing our expansion into more refined levels of consciousness; in all moments.

702. We release missing what is right in front of our nose; in all moments.

703. We release associating meeting other planetary species with engrams and muscle memory of being conquered; in all moments.

704. We release being quarantined from other planets due to our deficiencies in vibratory rate; in all moments.

705. We upgrade our DNA to thrive within intergalactic relationships; in all moments.

706. We remove all blockages to upgrading Earth through the beneficial assistance of benevolent neighbors; in all moments.

707. We extract all mentalities that prevent us from graciously interacting with benevolent species; in all moments.

708. We dissipate all psychic intrusions that hold Earth in a tractor beam of fear and paralysis; in all moments.

709. We thwart all tendencies or propensities to be controlled by other species; in all moments.

710. We release inflicting our own fears and engrams on our relationship with other planets; in all moments.

711. We release emanating or resonating with intentions to plunder which keep us isolated from other planets; in all moments.

712. We upgrade Earth's understanding of its position regarding other planetary systems; in all moments.

713. We free Earth of all energies that has controlled or limited it; in all moments.

714. We release being controlled by worshiping a God that was inserted in our psyche; in all moments.

715. We remove all hypnotic suggestions from our psyche; in all moments.

716. We release all the pain, burden, and limitations that have been dumped on Earth; in all moments.

717. We release worshiping other planetary species that have enslaved us; in all moments.

718. We close off all our psychic airwaves from hypnotic intrusion; in all moments.

719. We remove all controlling devices of other planets from Earth; in all moments.

720. We nullify all contracts between Earth and any controlling planetary systems; in all moments.

721. We release the control wielded over Earth through limited belief systems; in all moments.

722. We take back from all other planetary systems all that they have taken from Earth; in all moments.

723. We remove all blockages to Earth being free of its most coarse vibrational tendencies; in all moments.

724. We remove all blockages to earth being a responsible and ethical neighbor to other planets; in all moments.

725. We remove all blockages to recognizing our kindred tribesman from other planets incarnated here on Earth; in all moments.

726. We shift our paradigm from feeling abandoned on Earth to recognizing our kindred spirits here in human form; in all moments.

727. We remove all curses on humanity; in all moments.

728. All of Earth transcends the victim consciousness; in all moments.

729. Earth transcends being dragged along in survival mode; in all moments.

730. Earth is centered and empowered in integrity, accountability, and valuing all life; in all moments.

731. All of Earth resonates, emanates, and is interconnected with all life in integrity, accountability, and valuing all life; in all moments and all dimensions.

Cults and
Personality Worship

Break up cults and personality worship by doing the following taps for yourself and as a surrogate for all of humanity. Say each statement three times while continuously tapping on the top of your head, a fourth time while continuously tapping on your chest, and a fifth time while continuously tapping on your abdomen. Take a deep breath after finishing the series.

732. We collapse and dissolve all cults; in all moments.

733. We collapse and dissolve all constructs that create and maintain demigods; in all moments.

734. We release worshiping cult leaders and celebrities like Gods; in all moments.

735. We release confusing powermongers for saints; in all moments.

736. We strip all illusion of grandeur off all powermongers and celebrities; in all moments.

737. We thwart any and all humans from being mesmerized by their own bullshit; in all moments.

738. We thwart all practices that day-trade in bullshit; in all moments.

739. We release the belief that repeating bullshit makes it true; in all moments.

740. We knock all powermongers off their pedestal; in all moments.

741. We hoist all powermongers, cult leaders and entitled celebrities on their own petard; in all moments.

742. We release elevating assholes to the status of saints; in all moments.

743. We dissipate all psychic streams of energy that propagate personality worship; in all moments.

744. We thwart encapsulating any individual in entitlement; in all moments.

745. We collapse and dissolve all hierarchies where the individual loses their empowerment; in all moments.

746. We strip all illusion off all personas that are a puppet for power; in all moments.

747. We send all energy matrices into the light and sound that use individuals to accrue and wield power; in all moments.

748. We command all complex energy matrices that use individuals to accrue and wield power to be escorted into the light and sound; in all moments.

749. We take back our energy from all personalities that are hard-wired into the psyche of the collective; in all moments.

750. We free all personalities that have been derailed from their spiritual journey by being worshipped; in all moments.

751. We thwart all individuals avoiding their own accountability by fixating on worshipping a personality; in all moments.

752. We strip all illusion off the belief that any outer faction or person is going to save us; in all moments.

753. We free all humans from the painfully slow learning curve in awakening to their own self-empowerment and accountability; in all moments.

754. We thwart all practices that cause humans to willingly or unwillingly give their energy away to personalities; in all moments.

755. We reclaim the sovereignty of all individuals that has been handed over to personalities; in all moments.

756. We release the compulsion of humans to want to be worshipped; in all moments.

757. We release humans striving to be worshiped out of desperation to be appreciated, validated, or loved; in all moments.

758. We remove all engrams and muscle memory of worshiping individuals; in all moments.

759. We dissipate all psychic streams of energy that elevate any human to the status of a saint; in all moments.

760. We thwart violating spiritual law by using one's eminence to profit off the gullibility or sincerity of individuals; in all moments.

761. We strip all illusion off all cults, their leaders and personality worship; in all moments.

762. We eliminate the first cause in any and all individuals using their innate likability to profit off others; in all moments.

763. We expose all cults and group settings of being the Ponzi scheme that they are; in all moments.

764. We collapse and dissolve all Ponzi schemes based on a charismatic personality; in all moments.

765. We return to all individuals all their lifeblood and sovereignty they have forfeited to a personality or cult; in all moments.

766. We release accepting hard-wired cults as untouchable; in all moments.

767. We remove all the pain, burden and limitations that cults and personalities have put on all humans in the collective; in all moments.

768. We extract all personality worship and hard-wired cults from our governing system; in all moments.

769. We immediately and thoroughly disarm, dismantle, delegitimize, dethrone, and deactivate all those who profit off their persona; in all moments.

770. We release mistaking anyone who talks to us through inner channels as a spirit guide; in all moments.

771. We release being coerced and manipulated by personalities from the other side who masquerade as spirit guides; in all moments.

772. All semantic infiltration traps are immediately collapsed and dissolved; in all movements.

773. We collapse and dissolve all hierarchies that trap humans in personality worship; in all moments.

774. We dissipate all the psychic layers of apathy that is built up from centuries of personality worship; in all moments.

775. We snap all people awake that were trapped in the apathy of personality worship; in all moments.

776. We immediately and thoroughly pull all individuals out of the stupor of personality worship; in all moments.

777. We pull all entrenched individuals out of apathy; in all moments.

Religious
Power Structures

Collapse religious power structures by doing the following taps for yourself and as a surrogate for all of humanity. Say each statement three times while continuously tapping on the top of your head, a fourth time while continuously tapping on your chest, and a fifth time while continuously tapping on your abdomen. Take a deep breath after finishing the series.

778. We release being prevented from accessing our own truth by religious mandates; in all moments.

779. We remove all fears ingrained in us by religions that disconnect us from our own sovercignty; in all moments.

780. We release being threatened by a vengeful and petty man-made God; in all moments.

781. We release being trapped in a stagnant state of consciousness by any religion; in all moments.

782. We remove ourselves from an apathy that a man-made heaven has immersed us in; in all moments.

783. We remove ourselves from a man-made hell that is entrenching us in outdated religious belief systems; in all moments.

784. We remove all individuals from all concepts of heaven and hell; in all moments.

785. We release being trapped in an outmoded belief system; in all moments.

786. We release foregoing our sense of reason to stay connected to the power structure of a particular religion; in all moments.

787. We release being abused by a petty vengeful God of man's making; in all moments.

788. We remove all the guardrails that religions have put on us to prevent us from exploring our own empowerment; in all moments.

789. We remove all engrams and muscle memory of being martyred to any and all religions; in all moments.

790. We remove all curses, threats, and blessings that all religions have put on us; in all moments.

791. We release the trauma of being sacrificed to God; in all moments.

792. We release being emotionally blackmailed by religions to keep us enslaved to their doctrine; in all moments.

793. We release the trauma, engrams, and muscle memory of fighting and dying in holy wars; in all moments.

794. We release being lost in cynicism and skepticism as lingering effects of religions; in all moments.

795. We release confusing Source for a petty man-made figure head of a religion; in all moments.

796. We release being hard-wired to any faction with a threatening personality at the helm; in all moments.

797. We release the fear of being ostracized, rejected, or abandoned by a religion; in all moments.

798. We release the trauma and spiritual paralysis that being ostracized from a religion has put on us; in all moments.

799. We release all internalized self-talk that was initiated by threats from clergy and religion factions; in all moments.

800. We release genuflecting before a man-made God; in all moments.

801. We release converting our spontaneous love for all life to synthetic robotic worship; in all moments.

802. We remove all the pain, burden, and limitations that all religious factions have put on all individuals; in all moments.

803. We give back to all humans all the joy, love, abundance, freedom, health, and wholeness that all

religious factions have taken from them; in all moments.

804. We release converting our organic zest for life into energetic tithing to any and all religious factions; in all moments.

805. We remove all curses and limitations that religious books, prayers, songs, and texts have put on us; in all moments.

806. We release resonating or emanating with any religious power structures; in all moments.

807. We extract all of humanity's sound frequency and light emanation from all religions; in all moments.

808. We thwart the practice of sending our energy out from the Earth and into space; in all moments.

809. We call back to Earth all the energy that humans have sent to a controlling faction; in all moments.

810. We replenish Earth with all the energy that was taken from it by beliefs in a heaven in the sky; in all moments.

811. We release perpetually cursing ourselves and others in humanity through repetitive curses called prayers; in all moments.

812. We strip all illusion off all practices that systemically dilute the sovereignty of humans; in all moments.

813. We release being trapped in the dark ages by the 'one life' belief system; in all moments.

814. All individuals are freed from factions that hard-wire and embed religious practices into life on Earth; in all moments.

815. We release being enslaved by our own ignorance; in all moments.

816. We strip all illusion off all versions of demigods, messiahs, saints, spirit guides, and mouthpieces for a man-made God; in all moments.

817. We release the fear of questioning entrenched religious factions; in all moments.

818. We release the practice of systemically profiting off human's desire to connect with Source; in all moments.

819. We release all forms of unworthiness and self-depravation that benefit the church's narrative; in all moments.

820. We take back our empowerment from all religious factions; in all moments.

821. We collapse and dissolve all opportunists and profiteers who use religion to deceive us; in all moments.

822. We remove all engrams and muscle memory of the belief that God hates us or is punishing us; in all moments.

823. We release being held in apathy by the indoctrination that suffering is God's will; in all moments.

824. We dissipate all psychic means of control that prevent us from experiencing our own empowerment; in all moments.

825. We release all the engrams, muscle memory, programming, conditioning, or belief systems that prevent us from claiming our empowerment; in all moments.

826. We release being distracted from our sovereignty through having a pissing contest with others' understanding of their man-made God; in all moments.

827. We free ourselves from all religious belief systems that fuel wars in the world; in all moments.

828. We free all woman from being subjugated by religions; in all moments.

829. We free all those who are gender fluid from being demonized by religions; in all moments.

830. We extract all the hypocrisy, arrogance, entitlement and self-serving interests that are reinforced through religions; in all moments.

831. Humanity and all individuals transcend religion and outer mandates; in all moments.

832. We extract a man-made God from our governing systems; in all moments.

Family
Power Structures

Overcome family power structures by doing the following taps for yourself and as a surrogate for all of humanity. Say each statement three times while continuously tapping on the top of your head, a fourth time while continuously tapping on your chest, and a fifth time while continuously tapping on your abdomen. Take a deep breath after finishing the series.

833. We release being told what to do; in all moments.

834. We release the trauma of being born to the enemy; in all moments.

835. We release feeling flawed or unworthy because of the family we were born into; in all moments.

836. We release the belief that all family relationships are love bonds; in all moments.

837. We remove all programming and conditioning that the family has indoctrinated into us; in all moments.

838. We release bending our will to the family dynamics; in all moments.

839. We release the trauma of our particular birth order; in all moments.

840. We remove all negative genetic propensities that show up in the family unit; in all moments.

841. We release giving our sovereignty over to family members; in all moments.

842. We release muting our light so as to not outshine family members; in all moments.

843. We release being programmed and conditioned to comply with family mandates; in all moments.

844. We dissipate all psychic streams of energy that profit off the illusion of strong family units; in all moments.

845. We release being trapped in organized religion by the family mandates; in all moments.

846. We release being scapegoated by the family; in all moments.

847. We release absorbing the apathy and ignorance of the family unit as part of our purpose; in all moments.

848. We release martyring ourselves to the family; in all moments.

849. We release needing to choose between the family and our own sovereignty; in all moments.

850. We remove all the engrams and muscle memory that the family unit has put on us; in all moments.

851. We release being trapped in the family; in all moments.

852. We remove all curses that the family has put on us; in all moments.

853. We release being defined by our family; in all moments.

854. We release all the regrets we have stored in regard to our family; in all moments.

855. We convert all the energy we have used in being embarrassed or resentful of our family into fuel to manifest our empowerment; in all moments.

856. We remove all the pain, burden, and limitations that the family has put on us; in all moments.

857. We take back all the joy, love, abundance, freedom, health, success, and wholeness that the family has taken from us; in all moments.

858. We release being at the mercy of the family dynamics; in all moments.

859. We free ourselves and all others from being trapped in family dynamics of jealousy, resentment, or obligation; in all moments.

860. We release being trapped in the confines of the family; in all moments.

861. We release feeling obligated to the family; in all moments.

862. We strip all illusion off our dynamics with the family; in all moments.

863. We release curbing our choices or preferences to leave the family; in all moments.

864. We nullify all contracts with all the family members; in all moments.

865. We release confusing love with karma; in all moments.

866. We release hating our children; in all moments.

867. We release the karma between ourselves and the family members we resent; in all moments.

868. We release confusing the family with our spiritual tribe; in all moments.

869. We erase all family karmic conditions from our soul contract; in all moments.

870. We release incarnating with the same family dynamics out of habit; in all moments.

871. We strip all illusion off the spiritual reason that we incarnated within a particular family; in all moments.

872. We release conforming to a patriarchal society; in all moments.

873. We release the reinforcement of a patriarchal society through the family unit; in all moments.

874. We release the belief that women are weak and helpless; in all moments.

875. We remove all engrams, muscle memory, and beliefs that women are less important than men; in all moments.

876. We release having society's invalidation of women play out in our family unit; in all moments.

877. We release preferential treatment and prejudices within the family unit; in all moments.

878. We release being scarred by the family; in all moments.

879. We release being trapped in the 'one life' belief system that obligates us to the present family unit; in all moments.

880. We remove all glass ceilings that the family has put on us; in all moments.

881. We shift our paradigm from living for the family to empowering ourselves; in all moments.

882. We transcend the karmic family; in all moments.

883. We strip all denial off ourselves in regard to the family; in all moments.

884. We choose love bonds; in all moments.

The Daisy of Death

Transcend the 'daisy of death' by doing the following taps for yourself and as a surrogate for all of humanity. Say each statement three times while continuously tapping on the top of your head, a fourth time while continuously tapping on your chest, and a fifth time while continuously tapping on your abdomen. Take a deep breath after finishing the series.

885. We release being trapped in the daisy of death; in all moments.

886. We release reinforcing the daisy of death with our thoughts, feelings, beliefs and actions; in all moments.

887. We collapse and dissolve the daisy of death; in all moments.

888. We shift humanity's paradigm from being trapped in the daisy of death to awakening to their innate empowerment and freedom; in all moments.

889. We release earth from being at the mercy of the daisy of death; in all moments.

890. We release confusing the daisy of death with the true flower of life; in all moments.

891. We transcend the daisy of death in favor of the true flower of life; in all moments.

892. We remove the lattice of time and space that is a construct of the daisy of death; in all moments.

893. We remove the lattice of limited belief systems that is a construct of the daisy of death; in all moments.

894. We remove the lattice of the universal mind that is a construct of the daisy of death; in all moments.

895. We remove the lattice of linear limitations that is a construct of the daisy of death; in all moments.

896. We remove the lattice of organized religion that is a construct of the daisy of death; in all moments.

897. We remove the lattice of hierarchies that is a construct of the daisy of death; in all moments.

898. We remove the lattice of human superiority that is a construct of the daisy of death; in all moments.

899. We remove the lattice of spiritual practices that is a construct of the daisy of death; in all moments.

900. We remove the lattice of all programming and conditioning that is a construct of the daisy of death; in all moments.

901. We remove the lattice of a 'one life' scenario that is a construct of the daisy of death; in all moments.

902. We remove the lattice of male superiority that is a construct of the daisy of death; in all moments.

903. We remove the lattice of degradation of goddess that is a construct of the daisy of death; in all moments.

904. We remove the lattice of the Roman Catholic Church that is a construct of the daisy of death; in all moments.

905. We remove the lattice of a man-made God that is a construct of the daisy of death; in all moments.

906. We remove the lattice of the quest for power that is a construct of the daisy of death; in all moments.

907. We remove the lattice of all autocrats that is a construct of the daisy of death; in all moments.

908. We remove the lattice of endless mind loops that is a construct of the daisy of death; in all moments.

909. We remove the lattice of all engrams of past-lives that is a construct of the daisy of death; in all moments.

910. We remove the lattice of romanticizing conspiracy theories that is a construct of the daisy of death; in all moments.

911. We remove the lattice of all religious books and scriptures that is a construct of the daisy of death; in all moments.

912. We remove the lattices of ignorance and apathy that is a construct of the daisy of death; in all moments.

913. We remove the lattice of the corporate world that is a construct of the daisy of death; in all moments.

914. We remove the lattice of religions that is a construct of the daisy of death; in all moments.

915. We remove the lattice of human arrogance and entitlement that is a construct of the daisy of death; in all moments.

916. We remove the lattice of psychic manipulation that is a construct of the daisy of death; in all moments.

917. We remove the lattice of the military industrial complex that is a construct of the daisy of death; in all moments.

918. We remove the lattice of inequality that is a construct of the daisy of death; in all moments.

919. We remove the lattice of misinformation that is a construct of the daisy of death; in all moments.

920. We release the lattice of akashic records that is a construct of the daisy of death; in all moments.

921. We remove the lattice of engrams of and muscle memory of war that is a construct of the daisy of death; in all moments.

922. We remove the lattice of history that is a construct of the daisy of death; in all moments.

923. We remove the lattice of all autocrats and powermongers that is a construct of the daisy of death; in all moments.

924. We remove the lattice of disparaging Earth that is a construct of the daisy of death; in all moments.

925. We remove the lattice of desecrating nature and natural resources that is a construct of the daisy of death; in all moments.

926. We remove the lattice of genocide that is a construct of the daisy of death; in all moments.

927. We remove all keystone issues from the lattice of the daisy of death; in all moments.

928. W remove the lattice of global warming that is a construct of the daisy of death; in all moments.

929. We remove the lattice of mass incarceration that is a construct of the daisy of death; in all moments.

930. We remove the lattice of addiction that is a construct of the daisy of death; in all moments.

931. We remove the lattice of the stronghold of power that is a construct of the daisy of death; in all moments.

932. We remove all lattices of platitudes that bury truth within the daisy of death; in all moments.

933. We remove the lattice of alien race distractions that is a construct of the daisy of death; in all moments.

934. We remove the lattice of ineptitude that is a construct of the daisy of death; in all moments.

935. We remove the lattice of all sabotages to the awakening of humanity that is a construct of the daisy of death; in all moments.

936. We remove all lattices of dark energy or nefarious intentions that is a construct of the daisy of death; in all moments.

937. We remove the lattice of bastardized sacred geometry that is a construct of the daisy of death; in all moments.

938. We strip all lattices that are a construct of the daisy of death; in all moments.

939. We release Earth from being perceived as a hopeless resting place for the unenlightened by awakened forms of life; in all moments.

940. We prove to interstellar species that Earth deserves to continue; in all moments.

941. We free Earth from being a favorite hangout for despots and powermongers; in all moments.

942. Earth and all its inhabitants are centered and empowered in enlightenment; in all moments.

943. Earth and all its inhabitants resonate, emanate, and are interconnected with all life in universal empowerment; in all moments.

New Age Practices

Transcend new age practices that are constructs of the daisy of death by doing the following taps for yourself and as a surrogate for all of humanity. Say each statement three times while continuously tapping on the top of your head, a fourth time while continuously tapping on your chest, and a fifth time while continuously tapping on your abdomen. Take a deep breath after finishing the series.

944. We release fixating on singular practices to exercise our empowerment; in all moments.

945. We release adopting new age practices to feel superior to others; in all moments.

946. We release playing out secret desires to be worshipped through new age practices; in all moments.

947. We release conjuring up old dynamics of power through new age practices; in all moments.

948. We release using new age practices to feel superior; in all moments.

949. We release using powerful methods to feel special; in all moments.

950. We close all portals to the dark arts; in all moments.

951. We nullify all contracts with dark forces; in all moments.

952. We release conjuring up old dynamics of power and intrigue using alternative practices; in all moments.

953. We release using props as a crutch for tapping into direct knowing; in all moments.

954. We release becoming imbalanced through smelling our own bullshit; in all moments.

955. We release pitting alternative practices against western medicine; in all moments.

956. We remove all pissing contests between new age practices and western medicine; in all moments.

957. We release desecrating what others believe; in all moments.

958. We strip all illusion off all those who dupe seekers through alternative practices; in all moments.

959. We release partaking of any healing practice from the superiority of male energy; in all moments.

960. We thwart all attempts by snake oil salesmen to deceive those who are desperate for assistance; in all moments.

961. We release getting trapped in taking on lower consciousness entities as advisors by believing they are spirit guides; in all moments.

962. We release confusing anyone who can talk to us through inner channels as spirit guides; in all moments.

963. We release opening the door to psychic attacks instigated by new age practices; in all moments.

964. We release being buried in platitudes regarding new age practices; in all moments.

965. We release trying to gain followers by using new age practices; in all moments.

966. We give back to all individuals all that was taken from them by opportunists who use new age practices; in all moments.

967. We remove all curses that we have put on all individuals through new age practices; in all moments.

968. We collapse and dissolve all energetic Ponzi schemes that have been created and maintained through new age practices; in all moments.

969. We thwart the use of Ouija boards as a children's game; in all moments.

970. We release the profiteering off the ignorance of others regarding new age practices; in all moments.

971. We release believing the loudest and most reinforced bullshit; in all moments.

972. We release hard-wiring bullshit into the collective through new age practices; in all moments.

973. We remove all blockages to perceiving in energy; in all moments.

974. We remove all blockages to perceiving from our more subtle senses of intuition, heart, and gut knowingness; in all moments.

975. We release allowing our ego or other peoples' egos to dupe us into unproductive practices; in all moments.

976. We release opening portals to the influence of dark energies; in all moments.

977. We release being blissfully ignorant in regard to channeling dark energies; in all moments.

978. We release partaking in mind altering drugs while engaging in alternative practices; in all moments.

979. We release the belief that mind alternating drugs can elevate you to higher consciousness; in all moments.

980. We free ourselves and all souls from being trapped in the lower astral plane; in all moments.

981. We release the belief that the lower astral plane is highest consciousness; in all moments.

982. We release strengthening the mind ego through mindless meditative practices; in all moments.

983. We release diluting our energy by practicing worship of any kind; in all moments.

984. We release the belief that it is possible to get beyond the realms of the mind using practices that are made of mind vibration; in all moments.

985. We free all souls that are trapped in the wasteland of the mental realms; in all moments.

986. We free all souls that are trapped in the wasteland of hallucinogenic states; in all moments.

987. We release the practices of the ignorant and naïve representing themselves as having mastered a craft; in all moments.

988. We strip all illusion off all those who lead others down dead end alternative paths; in all moments.

989. We free all the demigods, angels, saviors, and other personalities who have served their purpose and wish to be freed; in all moments.

990. We release leaning on renowned personas of different paths to prop ourselves up with the illusion of power; in all moments.

991. We forego the quest for power through alternative practices; in all moments.

992. We release sensationalizing those who have crossed over; in all moments.

993. We release breaking spiritual law by disturbing those who have crossed; in all moments.

994. We release using others' misfortune for our own entertainment or for profiteering; in all moments.

995. We release all cruelty and indifference to energies that are trapped in suffering; in all moments.

996. We free all energies that are trapped in suffering; in all moments.

997. We release inducing fear into others for entertainment or profit; in all moments.

998. We thwart all propensity to be a muse for nefarious intentions; in all moments.

999. We release cursing others by using our subtle senses to relay a message of fear to them; in all moments.

1000. We release all unethical practices in regard to the healing arts; in all moments.

1001. We release the belief that healing is not possible; in all moments.

1002. We remove all blockages to becoming our own healer; in all moments.

1003. We release falling prey to profiteers or opportunists; in all moments.

1004. We remove all blockages to operating in direct knowing; in all moments.

1005. We release needing a middle man to dispense truth to us; in all moments.

1006. We release doubting ourselves; in all moments.

1007. We are centered and empowered in operating from direct knowing; in all moments.

The Universal Mind

Transcend the universal mind by doing the following taps for yourself and as a surrogate for all of humanity. Say each statement three times while continuously tapping on the top of your head, a fourth time while continuously tapping on your chest, and a fifth time while continuously tapping on your abdomen. Take a deep breath after finishing the series.

1008. We thwart the worship of the universal mind; in all moments.

1009. We release confusing the universal mind with God; in all moments.

1010. We release being trapped in the mental realms by the universal mind; in all moments.

1011. We release all the suffering caused in the world through the universal mind; in all moments.

1012. We release being kept from our own empowerment by the universal mind; in all moments.

1013. We release emboldening autocrats and powermongers through the universal mind; in all moments.

1014. We remove all limitations that the universal mind has put on humanity; in all moments.

1015. We release being kept from our purpose by the universal mind; in all moments.

1016. We remove all misdirects from our empowerment that the universal mind has layered onto humanity; in all moments.

1017. We release feeding our life force into the universal mind; in all moments.

1018. We remove all the disingenuous and nefarious intentions that the universal mind has saddled on humanity; in all moments.

1019. We strip all illusion off the universal mind; in all moments.

1020. We extract all powermongers and profiteers from the helm of control through accessing the universal mind; in all moments.

1021. We gut the universal mind of all individual's and the collective's personal freedoms; in all moments.

1022. We remove all masks, walls, and armor from those who sit at the helm of control by hijacking the universal mind; in all moments.

1023. We remove all distortions of the collective that cause suffering and depravity through the universal mind; in all moments.

1024. We release sacrificing our creativity, imagination, and personal freedom to the universal mind; in all moments.

1025. We free humanity from being subjugated by the universal mind; in all moments.

1026. We release the fear of transcending the universal mind; in all moments.

1027. We free humanity from being petulant children at the mercy of the universal mind; in all moments.

1028. We free humanity from sitting at the feet of the universal mind; in all moments.

1029. We extract all vibrations of suffering and apathy from the universal mind; in all moments.

1030. We extract the vibrations of helplessness, victim consciousness, disease, and suffering from the universal mind; in all moments.

1031. We extract all layers of misunderstanding regarding Source from the universal mind; in all moments.

1032. We extract all Gods, personality worship, hierarchies of demigods, and self-serving operators from the universal mind; in all moments.

1033. We purge the universal mind of all misinformation and misunderstanding that prevents mass awakening; in all moments.

1034. We thwart the universal mind from stacking the deck against awakening; in all moments.

1035. We release the programming and conditioning that enables the universal mind from being beyond reproach; in all moments.

1036. We extract all catastrophic trajectories from the mandate of the universal mind; in all moments.

1037. We release the universal mind from becoming a profit sharing apparatus for powermongers and profiteers; in all moments.

1038. We thwart the universal mind from consuming the dreams and aspirations of the sincere; in all moments.

1039. We immediately and thoroughly purge the universal mind of all self-serving and nefarious intentions; in all moments.

1040. We free all humans from being pawns of mass enslavement because of the universal mind; in all moments.

1041. We thwart the inability of the masses to awaken through the glass ceiling of the universal mind; in all moments.

1042. We disconnect the controlling eye and all limiting forms of surveillance from the organic synergy of the collective; in all moments.

1043. We free all humans from being coerced, manipulated, and kept from their purpose through the universal mind; in all moments.

1044. We release dumbing down the synergy of the collective to the universal mind; in all moments.

1045. We release being derailed from the synergy of the collective by sabotages of the universal mind; in all moments.

1046. We remove all the pain, burden, limitations, and nefarious intentions that the universal mind has inflicted on the synergy of the collective; in all moments.

1047. The collective takes back all their joy, love, abundance, freedom, health, success, beauty, imagination, creativity, childlike wonder, peace, life, wholeness, sincerity, integrity, kindness, and empowerment from the universal mind; in all moments.

1048. The universal mind is collapsed and dissolved; in all moments.

1049. The ability to reason and expand through questioning is reinstated into the synergy of the collective; in all moments.

1050. The synergy of the collective is thwarted from giving away its power to the universal mind; in all moments.

The Ego

Transcend the ego by doing the following taps for yourself and as a surrogate for all of humanity. Say each statement three times while continuously tapping on the top of your head, a fourth time while continuously tapping on your chest, and a fifth time while continuously tapping on your abdomen. Take a deep breath after finishing the series.

1051. We release all imbalances through inflating the worth of the ego; in all moments.

1052. We release all imbalances through deflating the worth of the ego; in all moments.

1053. We release vacillating between arrogance and unworthiness; in all moments.

1054. We release forgoing our sovereignty to the ego; in all moments.

1055. We release elevating the apparatus of the ego to that of our sovereignty; in all moments.

1056. We release derailing our own empowerment by giving our sovereignty to the ego; in all moments.

1057. We release worshipping the ego; in all moments.

1058. We remove all veils to accessing our higher truth that the ego has laid upon us; in all moments.

1059. We release the belief that the ego is God; in all moments.

1060. We thwart the ego from controlling us by masquerading as our favorite saint, savior or spirit guide; in all moments.

1061. We release being demoralized by the ego; in all moments.

1062. We release the ego from preventing our transcendence by using our own akashic record to threaten us; in all moments.

1063. We release the inability to know when we are being tricked by the ego; in all moments.

1064. We release confusing tricks of the ego as demonic possession or entities; in all moments.

1065. We release being manipulated by the ego through obsessive thoughts; in all moments.

1066. We dissipate all psychic streams of energy of drama that the ego uses to distract us from our empowerment; in all moments.

1067. We release being distracted from our empowerment through the ego's use of the pleasure principle; in all moments.

1068. We remove all engrams and muscle memory of genuflecting before the ego; in all moments.

1069. We release being our own worst enemy through the ego; in all moments.

1070. We remove all engrams and muscle memory that the ego uses to keep us trapped in fear; in all moments.

1071. We release being trapped in the lower worlds by the ego; in all moments.

1072. We release being tricked into trapping ourselves into experiences by the ego; in all moments.

1073. We thwart the ego from taking pleasure out of our suffering; in all moments.

1074. We release being immersed in suffering to placate the ego; in all moments.

1075. We release being induced to fear to placate the ego's desire to exist; in all moments.

1076. We release the desecration of the sovereign self by the ego; in all moments.

1077. We release the ego's fear of being destroyed; in all moments.

1078. We release the ego-induced fear of being separated from our consciousness; in all moments.

1079. We release reverting to old consciousness by the ego; in all moments.

1080. We remove all the pain, burden, and limitations that we have inflicted on ourselves and others due to the ego; in all moments.

1081. We release all aversion to awakening; in all moments.

1082. We release being trapped in a 'one life' scenario by the ego; in all moments.

1083. We release having our communications with our higher self intercepted and sabotaged by the ego; in all moments.

1084. We release the ego interfering with our ability to remember our dreams; in all moments.

1085. We thwart the bastardization of truth by the ego; in all moments.

1086. We take back all the joy, love, abundance, freedom, health, success, and wholeness that the ego has taken from us; in all moments.

1087. We release being told we are crazy by the ego; in all moments.

1088. We prevent the ego from sabotaging our awakening; in all moments.

1089. We strip away all responsibilities that prevent our awakening; in all moments.

1090. We thwart all attempts of the ego to prevent us from accessing our subtle senses that allow us to perceive in energy; in all moments.

1091. We release the ego preventing us from accessing and accepting our own wisdom; in all moments.

1092. We strip all illusion off all the ego's attempts to subjugate us; in all moments.

1093. We release being a bitch to the ego; in all moments.

1094. We release agreeing to all the disparagement in the world that the ego tricked us in believing was truth; in all moments.

1095. We remove all blockages to accessing our own empowerment; in all moments.

1096. We take back control of our sovereign self from the ego; in all moments.

1097. We remove the ego from the helm of our Beingness; in all moments.

1098. We remove all the pain, burden, and limitations we have put on others due to the ego; in all moments.

1099. We give back to all others all the joy, love, abundance, freedom, health, success, and wholeness that we have deprived them of due to the ego; in all moments.

1100. We release allowing the ego to be a mouthpiece for our sovereign self; in all moments.

1101. We release placating others' egos by interacting with them ego to ego; in all moments.

1102. We release all the dances of the ego that we partake in; in all moments.

1103. We release the shameless stroking of the ego; in all moments.

1104. We transcend the systemic darkness and ignorance that the dance of the ego has kept us in; in all moments.

1105. We forgo the systemic dance of the ego that has overtaken humanity; in all moments.

1106. We release all fears of bowing out of the universal dance of the ego; in all moments.

1107. We release being demonized for refusing to partake in the dance of the ego; in all moments.

1108. We remove all the horrors that the dance of the ego has inflicted on humanity; in all moments.

1109. We free all humans from being derailed from their purpose by the systemic dance of the ego; in all moments.

1110. We transcend the dark ages by systemically ending the dance of the ego; in all moments.

Wake the Fⓐ#k Up

Accelerate universal empowerment by doing the following taps for yourself and as a surrogate for all of humanity. Say each statement three times while continuously tapping on the top of your head, a fourth time while continuously tapping on your chest, and a fifth time while continuously tapping on your abdomen. Take a deep breath after finishing the series.

1111. We release romanticizing drama and disease; in all moments.

1112. We release indulging on anything that deters us from awakening; in all moments.

1113. We release enjoying the orgy of our lower nature; in all moments.

1114. We release being trapped in tribalism; in all moments.

1115. We release the fear of being seen as less than perfect; in all moments.

1116. We release veering away from awakening by trying to be good; in all moments.

1117. We release denying any aspects of our lower nature; in all moments.

1118. We release the aversion to reading our akashic records to avoid culpability; in all moments.

1119. We release choosing the debauchery of operating from a base nature; in all moments.

1120. We release worshiping those who live in excess; in all moments.

1121. We release demonizing those who live in integrity and truth; in all moments.

1122. We release demonizing the avatars and those who have come here to serve; in all moments.

1123. We release denying our own empowerment to stay safe; in all moments.

1124. We remove all engrams and muscle memory that prevent us from embracing our empowerment; in all moments.

1125. We release giving our empowerment to powermongers and profiteers to use as they will; in all moments.

1126. We release creating stagnant layers of apathy and indifference through our refusal to engage our purpose; in all moments.

1127. We release the fear of speaking our truth; in all moments.

1128. We release confusing bullying, and unkindness with speaking our truth; in all moments.

1129. We release filtering truth through public opinion; in all moments.

1130. We release confusing opinions for truth; in all moments.

1131. We release getting pulled down in vibration by powermongers and profiteers who use us as energy generators; in all moments.

1132. We release indulging energy vampires out of politeness; in all moments.

1133. We slough of all archaic forms of decorum that leave us at the mercy of powermongers, profiteers, and opportunist; in all moments.

1134. We release being energetically raped by opportunists all with a smile on our face; in all moments.

1135. We release being programmed into lower consciousness through our choice of entertainment venues and subjects; in all moments.

1136. We release waiting; in all moments.

1137. We release being paralyzed through internalizing quaint notions like 'all in good time'; in all moments.

1138. We release being passive watchers of the dynamics of life through our complacency; in all moments.

1139. We remove all opinions that have been hard-wired into our psyche; in all moments.

1140. We remove all programming and conditioning that prevent us from accessing our empowerment; in all moments.

1141. We flush all toxic interaction from the sea of life; in all moments.

1142. We convert all nefarious intentions and their creations back into love, light and pristine music; in all moments.

1143. We release meditating in a toxic wasteland and believing it is pristine; in all moments.

1144. We release the sludge of ingrained bullshit from the psyche of the collective; in all moments.

1145. We thwart all attempts by powermongers, profiteers, or opportunists to feed off others; in all moments.

1146. We release the disconnect between cause and effect in all nefarious intentions; in all moments.

1147. We remove all engrams and muscle memory from all individuals and the collective that embolden hate; in all moments.

1148. We remove all blockages to transcending the worlds of duality; in all moments.

1149. We cleanse the collective of all the sludge that has collected on it and thwarted its empowerment; in all moments.

1150. We free humanity from the delusion of being saved by a third party; in all moments.

1151. We remove all symbology that hold us in romanticizing power and control; in all moments.

1152. We release the systemic practice of devaluing the moment; in all moments.

1153. We free all those trapped in matter, energy, space, and time; in all moments.

1154. We remove all blockages to seating ourselves at the sacred altar of the moment; in all moments.

1155. We transcend all the bullshit that has buried us in platitudes; in all moments.

1156. We remove all confusion between power and empowerment; in all moments.

1157. We give back to all individuals all the empowerment that has been taken from them; in all moments.

1158. We take back from all individuals all the power that they have taken from others; in all moments.

1159. We shift the paradigm of the collective from abusing power to owning its empowerment; in all moments.

1160. We thwart all attempts to rape anyone of their empowerment; in all moments.

1161. All of the world is centered and empowered in individual and universal empowerment; in all moments.

1162. All the world and all individuals resonate, emanate, and are interconnected with all life in empowerment; in all moments.

1163. We wake ourselves, all individuals, and the collective the f@#k up; in all moments.

JEN WARD

Jen Ward is a dynamic healer, performance coach, and group facilitator. She has devoted her life to helping others unlock their true potential. She is also an accomplished writer and poet.

Jen's extraordinary and challenging personal journey has gifted her with a unique ability to perceive in energy and read akashic records. This, along with her Spiritual Freedom Technique (SFT) tapping protocols, allows Jen to work with clients to remove blockages to happiness and effectiveness that exist within any individual.

Jen is the spiritual healer and inspiration behind Jarvin Media and its mission to ignite universal empowerment. She and her husband Marvin Schneider operate in synergy of purpose to uplift all of humanity.

MARVIN SCHNEIDER

Marvin Schneider is a strategy consultant, valuation expert, author, and speaker.

Marvin has dedicated his life to stimulating the transformation of the global business and investment communities to create wealth on an ongoing basis in ways that enhance the wellbeing of the individual, the wider community, and the environment. This purpose is underpinned by a noble intent to uplift all of humanity and bring the global business and investment communities into higher consciousness.

Marvin works in synergy with his wife Jen Ward to bring her spiritual insights, wisdom, and connection to Source to the mainstream through Jarvin Media.

www.ingramcontent.com/pod-product-compliance
Lightning Source LLC
Chambersburg PA
CBHW041820090426
42811CB00009B/1051